THE
EVERYTHING.
HOT SAUCE
BOOK

Dear Reader,

If you're reading this, you probably already have a favorite hot sauce. It's the one you reach for when you have eggs in the morning or when you're fixing yourself a late-night sandwich. It might be a well-known brand like Sriracha, or a lesser-known one like Secret Aardvark, or maybe it's a special concoction made from fresh chili peppers in your own kitchen.

If there is one thing I learned while writing this book, it's that people everywhere love their hot sauce. When I told folks—family, friends, random acquaintances—that I was writing a book about hot sauce, nearly everyone had the same reaction. Their eyes would light up immediately and they'd lean in, as if they were sharing a secret with me and say, "I have a great hot sauce that you should write about. It's my favorite. It's called . . . ."

Whether it's in Chicago, Accra, or Manila, hot sauce gets people's blood flowing and their mouths watering. While developing recipes for this book, my kitchen became home to dishes I never dreamed of making, from places like Ethiopia and Jamaica. Once I started exploring hot sauce, it both changed the way I cook and opened up a new world. I hope this book does the same for you.

Angela Garbes

Welcome to the EVERYTHING® Series!

These handy, accessible books give you all you need to tackle a difficult project, gain a new hobby, comprehend a fascinating topic, prepare for an exam, or even brush up on something you learned back in school but have since forgotten.

You can choose to read an *Everything*® book from cover to cover or just pick out the information you want from our four useful boxes: e-questions, e-facts, e-alerts, and e-ssentials.

We give you everything you need to know on the subject, but throw in a lot of fun stuff along the way, too.

We now have more than 400 *Everything*® books in print, spanning such wide-ranging categories as weddings, pregnancy, cooking, music instruction, foreign language, crafts, pets, New Age, and so much more. When you're done reading them all, you can finally say you know *Everything*®!

QUESTION

Answers to
common questions

FACT

Important snippets
of information

ALERT

Urgent
warnings

ESSENTIAL

Quick
handy tips

PUBLISHER Karen Cooper

DIRECTOR OF ACQUISITIONS AND INNOVATION Paula Munier

MANAGING EDITOR, EVERYTHING® SERIES Lisa Laing

COPY CHIEF Casey Ebert

ASSISTANT PRODUCTION EDITOR Melanie Cordova

ACQUISITIONS EDITOR Brett Palana-Shanahan

SENIOR DEVELOPMENT EDITOR Brett Palana-Shanahan

EDITORIAL ASSISTANT Ross Weisman

EVERYTHING® SERIES COVER DESIGNER Erin Alexander

LAYOUT DESIGNERS Colleen Cunningham, Erin Dawson, Elisabeth Lariviere, Denise Wallace

THE
EVERYTHING®
HOT SAUCE
BOOK

From growing to picking and preparing—
all you need to add some spice to your life!

Angela Garbes

Aadamsmedia
Avon, Massachusetts

To my family, old and new.

An Everything® Series Book.
Everything® and everything.com® are registered trademarks of F+W Media, Inc.

Published by Adams Media, a division of F+W Media, Inc.
57 Littlefield Street, Avon, MA 02322 U.S.A.
www.adamsmedia.com

ISBN 10: 1-4405-3011-4
ISBN 13: 978-1-4405-3011-1
eISBN 10: 1-4405-3065-3
eISBN 13: 978-1-4405-3065-4

Printed in the United States of America.

10 9 8 7 6 5 4 3 2 1

Library of Congress Cataloging-in-Publication Data
is available from the publisher.

This publication is designed to provide accurate and authoritative information with regard to the subject matter covered. It is sold with the understanding that the publisher is not engaged in rendering legal, accounting, or other professional advice. If legal advice or other expert assistance is required, the services of a competent professional person should be sought.

—From a *Declaration of Principles* jointly adopted by a Committee of the American Bar Association and a Committee of Publishers and Associations

Many of the designations used by manufacturers and sellers to distinguish their products are claimed as trademarks. Where those designations appear in this book and Adams Media was aware of a trademark claim, the designations have been printed with initial capital letters.

This book is available at quantity discounts for bulk purchases.
For information, please call 1-800-289-0963.

Contents

Introduction

IT'S HARD TO GET an exact number, but it's estimated that in the United States alone, bottled hot sauce sales exceed $200 million annually. Talk about something being on fire—and that's just in the United States. Americans are certainly not the only ones crazy about hot sauce. In fact, there's a worldwide love affair going on with the stuff. While no one actually knows the number of bottles of hot sauce sold around the world each year, we do know that nearly every country is home to multiple brands of sauce, not to mention markets and stores filled with fresh and dried chilies, chili powders, and spicy seasoning blends.

So, where does all this hot sauce come from?

The history of hot sauce begins with chili peppers. And, as you'll find out in this book, the history of chili peppers is a surprising and fascinating story that takes you all around the world. Chili peppers, also known as capsicums, originated in the Amazon jungles of South America, where they were grown and cultivated by native people for thousands of years before being "discovered" by Christopher Columbus in 1492.

It's crazy to think that just 500 years ago, no one outside of Central and South America had even seen or heard of a chili pepper. It's almost impossible to imagine what Indian curries and Szechuan stir fries tasted like before chilies found their way to Asia. But it didn't take long for chilies to unleash their addictive power around the world. They worked their way into the cuisine of nearly every country, then gave way to the birth of hot sauces, and, in the end, a booming multi-million dollar international industry.

Chili peppers and hot sauce are so popular because, simply put, they make everything taste better. Whether they are scorchingly hot or pleasantly mild, chilies and hot sauce add flavor and excitement to food. Even people who shy away from very spicy foods know that there is a distinct sensation that takes hold of your body when you eat chilies: They get your blood flowing, send your heart racing, and make your tongue wag. Sometimes it can be painful, but more often than not, chili peppers and hot sauce bring pleasure.

Gathering together with friends and family for a meal is already one of the most enjoyable and comforting things you can do. Around the world, every day—multiple times a day, in fact—people come together to break bread, talk, and laugh. And when you add the spice of chilies and hot sauce, things get even more fun. People's mouths tingle, they let down their guard, they're more likely to laugh—they feel even more alive.

The recipes in this book are designed to help you experience some of the joy chili peppers bring to people around the world. Because chilies exist in nearly every cuisine, be it Italian, Mexican, or Korean, recipe chapters are divided into different sections of the world to show you the breadth of the chili peppers' reach and influence. Use this book as a resource to explore foods that you might be unfamiliar with or curious about. There's one thing they all have in common: they're spicy as all get out.

On a practical note, cooking with spices like chili peppers and hot sauce is the easiest ways to add flavor to dishes without expending too much effort and, even better, without spending too much money. There are plenty of recipes in here for homemade hot sauces and spice mixes. Invest just a few dollars in making your own spicy sauces and seasoning blends to have in your refrigerator or pantry, and soon you'll be cooking up vibrantly flavored dishes that will impress both yourself and your guests with ease. So get cooking—and remember, these recipes are simply guidelines for you to follow. You can make things as spicy as you like, so don't be shy about experimenting and adding more hot sauce. Be bold!

CHAPTER 1

Chili Pepper History

Deep-fried, cheesy jalapeño poppers. Funky, fermented kimchi. Saucy, salty pasta puttanesca. What do these very different dishes from around the world have in common? They all share one common ingredient that gives them an unmistakably spicy kick: chili peppers. Over time, chili peppers and hot sauce have snuck their way into people's everyday lives. At nearly every meal, no matter where on earth you live, you'll find some form of chili peppers. For as much as people use chilies, though, most know very little about them. The history of chilies is a fascinating one, one that goes back thousands of years and is filled with thousands of varieties and a healthy dose of international intrigue.

What Is a Chili?

A *chili*, or *chili pepper*, as it is commonly called, is the fruit of any *capsicum* plant. *Capsicum* is a genus of plants in the Nightshade family called *Solanaceae*. Technical terms aside, what you really need to know is that Nightshades are a family of over 3,000 flowering plants that provide a number of foods essential to the human diet. The chili pepper is in good company, counting tomatoes, potatoes, eggplants, tomatillos, and huckleberries among its many edible relatives.

In the United States and Britain, chilies are referred to as peppers, but in other countries around the world such as Australia and India, they are called by their more official and scientific name: *capsicums*. Within the Capsicum genus, there are at least twenty known wild species and five domesticated ones. Each of these species is further subdivided into distinct varieties. There are literally thousands and thousands of varieties of capsicums, representing an incredible range of shape, size, color, and flavor. They run the gamut from fiery Thai bird chilies, about the size of your pinky finger, to decidedly mild bell peppers, which run about the size of your fist, with nearly every flavor and size in between.

QUESTION

Are chili peppers and peppercorns related?
No, chili peppers are completely different from peppercorns, which grow on trees. Confusing, no? You can blame it on Christopher Columbus, who mistakenly bestowed the name *pepper* on chilies because they had a spicy, hot flavor similar to that of black peppercorns with which he was already familiar.

One thing all capsicums do have in common, though, is that the fruits all start out green, then change color as they ripen. Some will stay green as they change to red or yellow, while others might turn white, purple, or orange. You can eat a capsicum at any stage of development, but sugars and other flavor compounds tend to accumulate during the final stages of ripening (the amount of Vitamin C also multiplies), so fully ripe peppers are tastier and more nutritious.

You've probably seen the strings of chili pepper Christmas lights sold in novelty stores—a length of green wire with glowing red chilies dangling off of them. It's actually very fitting: a chili pepper shrub, dark green leaves dotted with many bright fruits in shades like crimson, gold, violet, and orange does look like a plant that's been strung with festive lights. Some people even joke that capsicums are "nature's Christmas lights."

Capsicum Plants and Their Amazonian Jungle Origins

The story of chilies begins thousands of years ago, back in the B.C. era, deep in the humid heart of South America: the Amazon jungle. While the exact point of origin of chilies will always remain unknown, experts believe that it evolved in a lush rainforest area that is now Brazil, Bolivia, and Paraguay. Capsicums must love the sticky wet heat of this area because, to this day, it is still where the largest number of wild species grow.

FACT

Remarkably, though centuries have passed and many things have changed, chilies have managed to retain their original name. In Náhuatl, the language of the Aztec people, Native Americans called capsicum fruits *chilli*. The Spanish converted *chilli* to *chile*, and in English the word became *chili*. And so it is to this day.

It's estimated that chilies have been part of the human diet since at least 5000 B.C. By the time Columbus and his crew arrived in the New World in 1492, peppers had already spread from South America into Central America and what is now Mexico, as well as islands in the Caribbean. Native Americans were already cultivating and growing chilies as crops. In fact, all five of the domesticated forms we recognize today had already been developed. Cayenne, bell, and jalapeño—three of the most popular peppers today—were already thriving in Amazonia and beyond. The migration of these wild chilies throughout the region was not just the work of humans—birds also played a crucial role.

It's not hard to imagine how the bright red fruits of the capsicum plants, rising up out of vast patches of green, would catch a bird's attention. And because birds lack the receptor that detects the heat of capsicums, they, unlike humans, can ingest large quantities of chilies without breaking a sweat, needing a drink of water, or feeling any kind of pain or burn. After being ingested, capsicum seeds could be carried long distances inside a bird's stomach before falling to the ground in the form of bird droppings. After traveling hundreds of miles, chili seeds would fall from high up in the sky and land in fertile soil where the plants would quickly take root and flourish.

Chilies were destined for popularity. When Christopher Columbus arrived in the New World in 1492, chilies were already the most commonly used spice. Native Americans had domesticated at least four types of capsicums and people were drying chilies for easier transportation throughout the region. Given their widespread use and invigorating flavor, naturally Columbus didn't hesitate to load chilies onto his ships to take back to Spain.

The Chili's Journey to Europe

Columbus traveled to the Americas on behalf of the Spanish, who were in search of spices to help them compete with their trade rivals, the Portuguese. At the time the Portuguese had cornered the market on black pepper, which was highly prized and valuable. Despite a few mistakes and misunderstandings, Columbus's mission was a smashing success.

When Columbus arrived, his first mistake was believing that he had arrived in the East Indies (in reality, it was the Bahamas). He referred to the native people as *indios* (Spanish for Indians), even though they were actually Arawak, the indigenous people of the land. Second, upon tasting chilies and finding their flavor to be similarly spicy to black peppercorns, he dubbed the chilies *peppers*.

Once chilies hit the Iberian peninsula, both Spain and Portugal began trading them. Chili peppers spread through European ports, departing from Seville and Lisbon and arriving in other ports like Antwerp, Belgium. Western Europe is actually one of the only regions of the world that was slow to come around to the chili pepper. (Think about it: France, Germany, England, and Switzerland are known for many food items, hardly any of them spicy.) In fact, most of these countries did not begin using chili regularly as a spice until the nineteenth century.

FACT

> No ancient language—Arabic, Chinese, Persian, Hebrew, Greek, Sanskrit—has any word for *chili*. In fact, just over 500 years ago, no one in Europe, the Middle East, or Asia had ever seen or heard of chilies. Though hardly new to Native Americans, chilies are a "new world" offering that changed the world's culinary history forever.

Eastern Europe and the Mediterranean is a different story altogether. For starters, chilies took a more circuitous route to these areas. Instead of coming direct from Spain or Portugal, chilies were bought by Muslim merchants in India (more on this in a moment) and shipped, via the Persian Gulf or Red Sea, to Aleppo, Syria or Alexandria, Egypt, where they were then transported northward into Central and Eastern Europe. The path was roundabout, yes, but also so well established that for centuries many people in Europe were convinced that chilies originated in India.

The European country that embraced the capsicum with the most open arms, Hungary, did so only after Turkish invaders introduced it in 1526. The Turks, who went on to occupy Hungary for 150 years, brought with them chili peppers. Though Hungarians may have resented the Turkish presence, they fell in love with the chili peppers. The result? Hungary's famous paprikas, made from grinding dried bell and chili peppers. Paprika, which adds the color, flavor, and, some would say, soul to so many Eastern European dishes, ranges in flavor from mild and sweet to strong and spicy.

Chili's "World Domination"

While Columbus brought chilies back for the Spanish, it was their nemesis, the Portuguese, who are actually responsible for its global reach and influence. It was the Portuguese navy who had rounded south Africa's Cape of Good Hope and reached India in 1498, creating a perfect route for the chili pepper to go beyond South America and reach Asia and the Middle East.

In 1494, the Treaty of Tordesillas had essentially split control of the world in half between the Spanish and Portuguese empires, and the Portuguese did not waste any time exporting chili peppers from Brazil, the only part of South America that they controlled. By the early 1500s, they were regularly exporting large quantities of chili peppers to their African colonies, the Arab world, and beyond.

Africans were quick to adopt chili peppers, incorporating them into their diet immediately. African cuisine was already spicy, using native "grains of paradise," a ginger-like spice, so it's no surprise that people took to the chili pepper with enthusiasm. However, there was another, more insidious and intrusive element that also contributed to the chili pepper's rapid dispersal across the continent. The Portuguese were taking African slaves to work on their plantations in the New World and, as a way of trying to limit the possibility of slave uprisings and rebellions, they refused to bring a large group of people from just one community who would share a common language and culture. As a result, they traveled all over the continent to procure slaves—and they took chili peppers with them wherever they went. People were taken, but chili peppers were left behind. In a short time, chili peppers had spread from the islands of Cape Verde, off the coast of West Africa, all the way down to Mozambique.

African slaves are also responsible for bringing the chili pepper back to its American roots, taking chilies with them to plantations in the American south staring in the 1600s. The chili never quite migrated far enough north on its own to make it into what is now the United States. Instead the slaves, who also brought along the ingredients and dishes that make up the soul food of the south, brought it back closer to its original home.

The established Portuguese trading with India and Indonesia guaranteed the chili pepper's passage into Asia. India's adoption of chili peppers was so thorough, their cuisine so quickly entrenched in its flavors, that for many years people—even botanists—believed that the chili must be native to the country. Soon, chili peppers made their way to China.

While the Portuguese surely brought chili peppers to China, they may not have been the first. It's possible that Indian and Arab traders had already done so before any Europeans arrived. In China, chili peppers were embraced particularly well by people in the Hunan and Szechuan provinces. To this day, Szechuan cuisine is known for its fiery flavor and frequent use of chili peppers. It's probably not just coincidence that these two provinces are located on an ancient silk trading road that linked India to China before coastal port trading.

After China, chili peppers spread throughout Asia to countries like the Philippines, Japan, Thailand, and Korea. It's right about this point, though, that things get a little fuzzy. Because there were so many trade routes and ships—Japanese, Indian, Spanish, Portuguese, Chinese—it's hard to know exactly who brought what to whom, let alone when. But one thing is for certain: Everyone welcomed the chili pepper.

Modern Chili Cultivation and Commerce

Columbus was eager to take the chili back to Spain and, it turns out, Spain and the rest of the world were even more eager to embrace it. The popularity of chilies—and the rapid rate at which they caught on across the globe—cannot be overstated. Within fifty years of Columbus bringing peppers back to Spain, chilies were being cultivated in Central Europe, the Balkans, Italy, the Middle East, China, India, and all across Africa. Today it may be the most widely used spice in the world. It's definitely high on the list.

Chili farming and distribution today has become a big business, accounting for millions of dollars in commerce across the entire globe. Chili peppers are grown commercially in over eighty countries, primarily warm climates, with over 3,000 square miles dedicated to their cultivation. The largest harvests come from India, Mexico, and China.

India is the world's largest producer of chili pepper, accounting for 45 percent of the world's area and 25 percent of its production. It's also the largest consumer and exporter of chili peppers today. The country exports over 51,900 tons of chili peppers annually and produces close to 8 million tons of dried chilies a year.

The economy of chili peppers extends well beyond the fresh fruit of the capsicum. Chilies are available in a multitude of forms including fresh, dried, and powdered. It is also commonly sold as oleoresin capsicum, a naturally occurring combination of oil and resin that is extracted from the plant and used to impart the peppery power and flavor to a number of products. Chilies are now even part of people's décor. You've no doubt seen *ristras*, strings of dried chilies adorning restaurants, doorways, and kitchens around the world.

FACT

The United States is getting spicier every year. The consumption of spices in the United States has grown almost three times as fast as the population over the past several decades. Or to put in another way: compared to the 1970s, Americans now consume 600 percent more chili peppers. An influx of immigrants—from Mexico, Southeast Asia, and India—and different cuisines is the main reason things have heated up.

You need not look any further than your local supermarket to see the tremendous power of chili peppers. Where you once may have found just red and green bell peppers, you'll now find jalapeños, serranos, habaneros, Thai bird, Scotch bonnets, New Mexicos, and Anaheims. Then there are the dried red pepper flakes, cayenne pepper, chili pepper, and chipotles. And that's just the tip of the iceberg. A walk down the condiment aisle would reveal a whole other world that you'll soon be exploring: hot sauce.

CHAPTER 2

Getting Hot in Here: The Chili Pepper Effect

Chili peppers are the only food item that can cause both intense pleasure and intense pain. Perhaps this is what makes them so popular worldwide? Eating chilies can elicit responses ranging from sweating, burning, shouting, and crying, yet millions of people around the world choose to do it over and over, every day. And it's not just humans who are hooked on capsicums: Studies show that chimpanzees, rats, goats, and dogs may also become addicted to chilies. It's time to delve into the science behind the mysterious power these fruits hold.

Anatomy of a Chili

Before you delve into the wonderful world of cooking with chilies, it would be most helpful to understand the anatomy of the chili, the integral parts of this plant that lead to the magical heat.

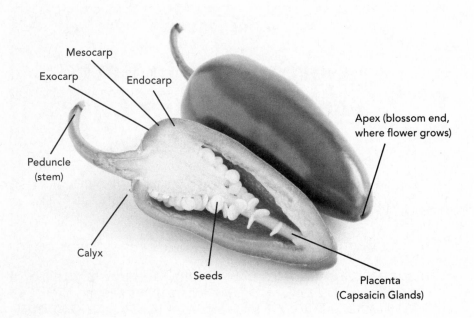

Capsaicin Glands

This is where the magic happens. The capsaicin gland produce capsaicin, the substance that gives chili peppers all of their fire. The glands are located at the top of the pepper, close to the stem and lie in between the pepper's placenta and endocarp.

Placenta

The placenta is the part of the pepper to which the seeds are attached. They are found at the top of the pepper, close to the stem. The placenta, also called the ribs, are white and are quite spicy. Removing the placenta from a chili will remove much of its heat.

Seeds

Seeds are often cut out of chili peppers, along with the placenta, to alleviate the amount its level of spiciness. While seeds do not produce capsaicin, they are so close to the capsaicin glands that they absorb a lot of their heat.

Peduncle

The peduncle is the botanical term for the stem of the chili pepper. It links a chili to the plant's branch and is green, fibrous, and woody.

Calyx

The calyx, also called the crown, is the remnant of the flower from which the chili grew. It is found at the base of the stem and is the transition between that woody part and the juicier fruit of the plant.

Skin

The skin of the chili pepper is comprised of three sections: the exocarp, mesocarp, and endocarp. The exocarp is the outermost layer of the pepper, the only "skin" that is visible when you look at a pepper whole. The mesocarp is the thicker, fleshy middle layer of skin. The mesocarp contains the highest amount of water and provides the chili pepper with structural support. It is this layer that gives chilies their crispness. The endocarp is the innermost layer that surrounds the seeds. It is combined mainly of membranes and is very thin.

Apex

The apex is the bottom tip or blossom end of the chili pepper. It is the least spicy section of the pepper and contains the smallest amount of capsaicin.

What Makes a Chili Hot?

The heat in chilies comes from a chemical compound called *capsaicin*. *Capsaicin* is an alkaloid that, while lacking any distinct flavor or color, is so potent it can withstand long periods of drying, freezing, and heating or cooking without losing any of its strength. Capsaicin is so potent that it can actually be detected by the human tongue even if it has been diluted in a solution of one million units of liquid to one part capsaicin.

There are other chemical compounds, collectively called *capsaicinoids*, found in chilies but the best known—not to mention the most pungent—is capsaicin. Capsaicin, appropriately, is produced in the capsaicin glands in the placenta of each chili pepper.

Pure capsaicin can cause severe burns when it comes into contact with human skin. In laboratories where they deal with crystalline forms of capsaicin, workers must wear full face masks and full body suits to prevent injuries that would be caused by direct contact and inhalation.

How Capsaicin Works

Capsaicin triggers pain receptors in the mouth and nose. This is what causes the burning feeling on your tongue and mouth, maybe even a little sneezing. When your brain receives the message—"Pain! Hot! Hot! Hot!"—it releases a chemical *Substance P* to counteract the pain. If you expose yourself to capsaicin repeatedly, which most people do, you will eventually develop a higher threshold for pain and a lower sensitivity to the spice. So if you find, over time, that you want even spicier foods, it's likely because you've built up a tolerance for chilies.

FACT

If you think your job is sometimes painful, try picking chili peppers for a living. *Hot hands* is a commonly reported ailment among Tabasco chili pickers. Tabascos must be picked when they are ripe, which means they are more likely to break, which in turn releases a flood of capsaicin over workers' hands. Many Tabasco pickers suffer from hands that constantly tingle with a bit of pain and heat.

In addition to Substance P, the body also releases a rush of endorphins—natural painkillers that can also produce a feeling of euphoria. Eating chilies produces the same blissful feeling that exercise (ever heard of *runner's high*?), excitement, and orgasms do. So with chilies, pain and pleasure go hand-in-hand and the overall sensation is one that is downright addictive.

Measuring Heat with the Scoville Scale

Chili pepper heat is measured in Scoville Heat Units (SHU). The Scoville scale was first developed in 1912 by a Detroit chemist named Wilbur Scoville. Scoville designed a basic test to measure the heat of chili pods, originally calling it the *Scoville Organoleptic Test*. Here's how it worked: Scoville blended pure ground chilies then added them to sugar water, which was then tasted by a brave panel of people. Tasters measured the point at which the chili extract could no longer be detected in water. The amount of dilution became the chili heat rating. If the dilution consisted of one part chili extract to 350 parts water, the chili was rated at 350 Scoville Heat Units. The rates ranged from 0 for bell peppers to 350 for habaneros.

QUESTION

Who Was Wilbur Scoville?
Wilbur Lincoln Scoville was born in Bridgeport, Connecticut on January 2, 1865. While working for the Parke-Davis Pharmaceutical Company, now a subsidiary of Pfizer, Scoville developed the earliest version of what is now the standard for measuring the intensity of chili peppers. During his career, Scoville published two books, *The Art of Compounding* and *Extracts and Perfumes,* and was awarded the Ebert prize from the American Pharmaceutical Association in 1922. In 1929 he received the Remington Honor Medal and also received an honorary Doctor of Science from Columbia University.

If this sounds like an imperfect, problematic system to you, that's because it was. The simplicity of the original Scoville Test was also what made it problematic. As a taster's pain receptors became less sensitive to the capsaicin, the harder it was to gauge the chili's heat. The system also did not account for some people simply having higher tolerances for heat than others.

These days, while still using Scoville Heat Units, measuring a chili's potency is now a much more precise and scientifically sound process. Thanks to something called High Pressure Liquid Chromatography, a fancy process developed in the 1970 to separate chemical compounds, which provides a reading of capsaicin units in a solution. This system requires expensive equipment, but now the results are much more accurate and reliable.

FACT

In its purest form, capsaicin is rated at 16,000,000 Scoville Heat Units. Here's an idea of how some other chilies measure up: the Naga Jolokia or Ghost Pepper comes in at 800,000–1,000,000 SHU; Scotch bonnets 150,000–325,000 SHU; and Jalapeños 2,000–5,000. Bell peppers bring up the rear with 0.

Since many factors affect chili heat, though, it is impossible to make measuring chili heat an exact science. Chilies grown in warmer climates tend to be hotter, even if they are the same variety as ones grown in colder areas. Also, two peppers from the same variety—even from the same farm or plant—can vary widely in heat. For this reason, chilies are typically sold and labeled with a range of minimum and maximum SHU.

Health Benefits and Medicinal Uses of Chilies

From a health standpoint, chilies are quite good for you. So eat away! No need to feel guilty. Capsicums contain large amounts of the vitamins C and A. (Fresh red chilies actually contain as much vitamin A as carrots.) Chilies also contain healthy doses of vitamin E and potassium. Measured by weight, fresh peppers actually have close to three times as much vitamin C as lemons, limes, and oranges. Chili peppers are also rich in antioxidants, which soak up free radicals. And it doesn't matter what type of chili pepper you favor—the nutritional value is roughly the same in every pepper, regardless of the variety.

Capsaicin is also used in skin liniments to remove the sting of skin irritations and the pain of nerve conditions like shingles. On the skin, capsaicin destroys Substance P, the pain reducing substance produced by the body, as it is drawn to the site of irritation. The body sends more Substance P, and capsaicin destroys it all until the supply is depleted and the burning sensation is gone. Other liniments contain oleoresin capsicum, a naturally derived resin from capsicums, to produce a localized heat effect that increases blood flow to sore areas.

A growing number of capsicum-based products such as Sinus Buster are available on the market to relieve things like chronic congestion and headaches. While you may not be prescribed chilies by a doctor, studies do show that chilies affect people's moods. The endorphins released create an overall feeling of well being, so you might turn to chilies for just a little psychological and emotional pick-me-up. Capsaicin will also be tested to treat *diabetic neuropathy* (the pin-pricking, burning sensation on the bottoms of the feet that many diabetics suffer from) as well as rheumatoid arthritis.

ALERT

While not all the purported health benefits have been proven by scientific method, the list of alleged benefits includes: circulation stimulation, boosted metabolism, relief from migraines, aid in fighting cancer cells, lowering blood pressure, losing weight, and increasing heart health.

Other Uses of Chilies

Aside from their health and medicinal uses, chilies and capsaicin are put to work in a wide range of products. Currently, there are around 1,200 patented products using capsaicin or chili peppers, mostly as deterrents for both people and pests. Chilies lend their bite to insecticides, spider inhibitor sprays, pepper sprays, and disinfectants.

Capsaicin is the main component in self-defense anti-aggressor sprays like pepper spray. Originally developed in the 1960s as Halt Animal Repellent, pepper spray has now evolved into a product used by both women and men to drive off would-be attackers. Capsaicin can be painful when it makes contact with skin, but it is even more devastating if it gets into eyes or mucus membranes such as nostrils. If pepper spray is inhaled, it will disperse into small particles, giving assailants a lot of trouble breathing. The United States Postal Service gives its carriers a spray to deter dogs that is made from a synthetic substance modeled after capsaicin.

Chili plants likely developed capsaicin as a natural defense against animals eating their fruit. People have taken this lesson in evolution and applied it to their own yards as an animal deterrent. If you have a bird feeder whose seeds seem to be feeding more squirrels than birds, spraying it with a capsaicin-laced solution should be enough to keep away those pesky little animals. Likewise, if deer are invading your garden or eating away the shrubs and trees in your lawn, spraying them with liquid containing capsaicin will be effective in keeping them away. Deer have highly developed senses of taste and smell and will certainly avoid a potent irritant such as capsaicin.

Along with keeping some animals away, capsaicin also provides other animals with relief. Capsaicin is proven to provide hypersensitizing and pain relieving properties in animals such as horses. For this reason, it is now a banned substance in equestrian sports. At the show jumping events of the 2008 Summer Olympics, four horses tested positive for the substance and were disqualified.

CHAPTER 3

Types of Chilies: Around the World with the Five Domesticated Species

Chili peppers come in a seemingly endless assortment of flavors, shapes, sizes, and colors. There are literally thousands of types of chilies and it's exactly this variety that helps make them so popular the world over. Mild, green shishito peppers are beloved in Korea and Japan; padron and piquillo peppers are synonymous with Spain, and Mexico is known for its chipotles, guajillos, and chiles de arbol. A quick, round-the-world tour of the five domesticated chili species gives a vibrant picture of some of the world's favorites.

Capsicum Frutescens

Peppers of the capsicum frutescens species are typically small and quite spicy. Its most famous pepper is the tabasco, which is used to make Louisiana's famous Tabasco sauce. This species is a decidedly international traveler, with the piri piri being popular in East Africa, and the japone being used widely in Chinese, Thai, and Japanese cooking. Frutescens are also often grown as ornamental plants because they bear large quantities of cute, stand-up-straight peppers in a number of bright colors.

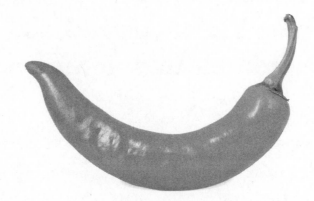

The classic Tabasco chili

▼   **CAPSICUM FRUTESCENS**

Name	Color	Heat Level (Scoville Heat Units)	Average Size
Tabasco	light yellow, ripens red	30,000–50,000 SHU	1–1.5" long, 1 cm wide
Thai Bird's Eye	green, ripens to red	50,000–100,000 SHU,	1" long, .5 cm wide
Piri Piri	green, ripens to purple or red	50,000–175,000 SHU	4" long, 1" wide
Malagueta	green, ripens to red	60,00–100,000 SHU	2" long, .5" wide
Japone	red	20,000–25,000 SHU	1–3.5" long, .5" wide
Bangalore Torpedo	lime green, ripens to red	16,000–50,000 SHU	5" long, .5" wide
Dagger Pod	green, ripens through orange to red	30,000–50,000 SHU	4" long, .5" wide
Kambuzi/Malawian	yellow, orange, red	50,000–175,000 SHU	1–1.5" long, 1.5" wide

Capsicum Chinense

Mistakenly dubbed *Chinese* by Dutch physician Nikolaus von Jacquin in 1776, capsicum chinense peppers are actually native to the Americas. They are both loved and feared for their fiery heat. These peppers are used widely throughout the cuisine of the Yucatan Peninsula of Mexico and the Caribbean Habaneros, Scotch bonnets, and Ghost Peppers—Chinense peppers are not for the faint of heart or the weak-tongued.

The Habanero

▼   CAPSICUM CHINENSE

Name	Color	Heat Level (Scoville Heat Units)	Average Size
Habanero	green, ripens to orange or red	200,000–300,000 SHU	1–1.5" long, 1–1.5" wide
Scotch bonnet	green, ripens to bright orange and red	100,000–350,000 SHU	1–1.5", 1–1.5" wide
Naga Jolokia (Ghost Pepper)	green, ripens to deep red	800,000–1,000,000 SHU	2.5–3" long, 1–1.5" wide
Madame Jeanette	yellow, bright red	175,000–225,000 SHU	2.5" long, 1–1.5" wide
Hainan Yellow Lantern	yellow	175,000–350,000 SHU	2" long, 1" wide
Aji Dulce	green, ripens to red	200,000–350,000 SHU	1" long, 2" wide
Facing Heaven	bright red	200,000–500,000 SHU	2.5" long, 1.5" wide
Datil	dark yellow and orange	200,000–300,000 SHU	3" long, .5" wide
Habanero Red Savina	red	350,000–575,000 SHU	2" long, 1.5" wide

▼ **CAPSICUM CHINENSE**

Name	Color	Heat Level (Scoville Heat Units)	Average Size
Jamaican Hot Chocolate	chocolate brown when ripe	100,000–200,000 SHU	2.5" long, 1.5" wide
Paper Lantern Habanero	lime green, orange, bright red	300,000–500,000 SHU	2" long, .5–1" wide
Aji Limo	yellow, ripens through purple and orange to red	50,000–60,000 SHU	2" long, 1.5" wide

FACT

Currently, the Guinness World Record for hottest known chili pepper is held by the Trinidad Scorpion "Butch T," grown by The Chilli Factory in Australia and rated at 1,463,700 Scoville Heat Units (SHU) on March 1, 2011. Previous peppers with this dubious distinction include the Bhut Jolokia Pepper and the Naga Viper.

Capsicum Annuum

Capsicum annuums are the most common and extensively cultivated of all chili peppers. Annuums run the gamut from bell peppers to milder peppers like jalapeño, Anaheim, poblano, New Mexico, and Hungarian wax. Although the species name means *annual*, these plants are not annual plants. In fact, if they grow in a warm enough place without harsh winters, the plant can live for several years and become a perennial that bears fruit for multiple years. Annuums are also the easiest species of peppers for amateur gardeners to grow.

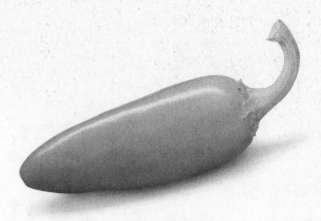

Whole Jalapeño

▼   **CAPSICUM ANNUUM**

Name	Color	Heat Level (Scoville Heat Units)	Average Size
Jalapeño	green, ripens to red	2,000–5,000 SHU	2.5–3" long, 1–1.5" wide
Poblano	dark, deep green	1,000–2,000 SHU	4.5" long, 1.5–2" wide
Anaheim	light green	500–2,500 SHU	6–7" long, 1.5–2" wide
New Mexico	dark green, ripens to bright red	1,000–1,500 SHU	4–6" long, 1–1.5" wide
Serrano	green, ripens to red	8,000–22,000 SHU	3" long, .5" wide
New Mexico Big Jim	green, ripens to red	500–1,000 SHU	8–10" long, 2.5–3" wide
Casabella	yellow, red	1,500–4,000 SHU	1.5" long, .5" wide
Bola	red	1,000–2,500 SHU	1.5" long, 1.5" wide
Cayenne	red	30,000–50,000 SHU	4" long, .5-1" wide
Charleston Hot	green, ripens to bright orange	80,000–100,000 SHU	3" long, .5" wide
Cherry Bomb	green, ripens to bright red	2,500–5,000 SHU	2" long, 3" wide
De Arbol	red	15,000–30,000 SHU	3" long, .5" wide
Fresno	green, ripens to bright red	3,000–8,000 SHU	3" long, 1" wide
Goat Horn	green, ripens to bright red	5,000–8,000 SHU	5–6" long, 1" wide
Hungarian Yellow Wax	yellow, ripens to orange-red	2,000–4,000 SHU	5" long, 1" wide
Pepperoncini	green, ripens to red	100–500 SHU	3.5" long, 1" wide

Name	Color	Heat Level (Scoville Heat Units)	Average Size
Piquin	red	30,000–40,000 SHU	1" long, .5" wide
Padron	green	1000–1,500 SHU	4" long, 1–1.5" wide
Shishito	green, ripens to red	1,000–2,000 SHU	3.5" long, .5–1" wide
Thai Dragon	green, ripens to red	75,000–100,000 SHU	2–3" long, .5" wide

Capsicum Pubescens

Peppers from the capsicum pubescens species are not very well known outside of Central and South America. The name *pubescens* refers to the hairs that grow on the underside of the plant's leaves. Unlike all other chilies, the seeds of pubescens are black and cannot be cross-pollinated with any other varieties. This might explain why there are far fewer of this species and why they are not as widespread around the world. These plants and peppers are quite hale and hardy, withstanding lower temperatures and surviving at higher altitudes. The fruits are thick-skinned, like bell peppers, and apple shaped.

The Rocoto Pepper

▼ **CAPSICUM PUBESCENS**

Name	Color	Heat Level (Scoville Heat Units)	Average Size
Rocoto	green, ripens to red	225,000–350,000 SHU	2–3" long, 1" wide
Manzano	green, ripening to yellow, orange, and red	12,000–30,000 SHU	1.5–2" long, .5–1" wide

Capsicum Baccatum

The name *baccatum* refers to the small berry-like fruits that flourished in this species' wild chilies. The fruits of the domesticated variety we see on the market today, however, have been purposefully cultivated and are not as small and round. These peppers, particularly the aji amarillo, are a staple of Peruvian cuisine and are seen primarily in this region of South America.

Aji Pepper

▼ **CAPSICUM BACCATUM**

Name	Color	Heat Level (Scoville Heat Units)	Average Size
Aji	yellow, ripens to orange	40,000–50,000 SHU	4" long, 1" wide
Aji Cereza	bright red	70,000–80,000 SHU	1" long, 1" wide
Peppadew	green, ripens to bright red	1,000–5,000 SHU	1" long, 1" wide
Brazilian Starfish	red	5,000–20,000 SHU	1" long, 2" wide
Christmas Bell	red	100–500 SHU	2" long, 1.5" wide

Fresh Chilies and Their Dried Counterparts

Did you know that a chipotle chili is actually a smoked and dried jalapeño? Or that an ancho chili is just a dried poblano? The art of drying chilies has been around as long as chilies themselves. Drying was an early method of preserving chilies and it also made it much easier to transport over long distances. The true beauty of drying, though, is that chilies take on whole new flavors and scents that allow them to be used in a new set of preparations. Much of Mexican cuisine—moles, powders, and sauces—is based on dried chilies and different combinations thereof. Sauces may be as simple as one chili blended with spices, or as complicated as four or five chilies blended with other seasonings.

Dried Chili Basics

The following is a basic introduction to some of the most commonly used dried chilies. You'll find out what fresh chilies they originate from as well information on their distinct flavors and uses. The more you begin using dried chilies, the more attuned you will become to their subtle (and not so subtle) differences in flavor. You'll probably find yourself reaching for them more and more, as they add a wonderful depth of flavor to food, and experimenting with different recipes and combinations.

Ancho

Ancho chilies, which are ripe, red poblano chilies that have been dried, are the most commonly used dried chili in Mexican cuisine. Anchos are fairly mild, with just a little heat, with a pleasant almost raisin-like aroma. They are reddish brown with wrinkled skin and a little bit of shine. Anchos are typically lightly toasted to help release their oils and then soaked. After, they are ground smooth with other ingredients for cooked sauces such as adobo.

Cascabels

Cascabels are small, round chilies with dark reddish-brown skin. They are typically about 1" long and a little over 1" in diameter, with a good amount of heat and an earthy, rich flavor. The name cascabel means rattlesnake, and it's called this because when you shake the pepper, the seeds inside rattle.

Chipotle

Chipotle might be the most famous dried chili outside of Mexico, which is appropriate since it is really a jalapeño, one of the most recognized peppers in the world. Chipotles are simply red, ripened jalapeños that are smoked and dried. They are pretty small (picture a shriveled jalapeño), with a light-brown skin and a rather spicy, smoky flavor. The name comes from the Náhuatl Indian words *chil* (chili) and *poctli* (smoke).

De Arbol

Chiles de arbol are long, skinny chilies that grow not from a tree (as the word *arbol* might suggest), but from a shrub. They begin green, but ripen to a solid red, which fades slightly after they are dried. Chiles de arbol are very hot with a distinct, pleasantly bitter flavor. They're often toasted and ground to make sauces, and make a wonderful salsa when combined with roasted tomatillos.

Guajillo

Guajillos are one of the most commonly used dried chilies throughout Mexico because they are widely available and cheap to grow. Guajillos are mirasol chilies that have been dried, and they have a smooth, dark red—almost purple—skin. Guajillos are up to 5" long and about 1½" wide. They have a medium-to-hot level of spice and a clean, bright flavor. Typically they are soaked and then blended with other ingredients to make a cooked sauce for meats.

Pasilla

Pasilla chilies are chilaca chilies that have been allowed to fully ripen, after which they are dried. They are long and skinny (roughly 6" by 1" wide) with a waxy, nearly black surface with plenty of deep wrinkles. pasillas have a deep chili flavor and a medium level of heat. Typically, pasillas are toasted, then soaked and then blended with other ingredients in cooked sauces. They are particularly good with seafood and are often combined with ancho chilies.

CHAPTER 4

Growing Your Own:
A Guide to Chili Pepper Plants

It's easy enough to go to your local supermarket or green grocer and pick up fresh chilies. These days just about every store stocks at least three different varieties. But die-hard chili fans should really consider growing their own. There's something inherently satisfying about nurturing a plant from its early stages into a full, fruit-bearing bush. Also, ask anyone with a garden: Food magically tastes better when you grow it yourself. There's nothing as delicious as using your freshly picked chilies to make a quick salsa that you can devour just minutes later.

Choosing What Chilies to Grow

If you want to grow your own chilies, there are a few things to consider: You'll need a little bit of space, good soil, and ample sunlight. Chilies will grow better in some areas of the country than others, and you're likely to have more success with certain varieties, but it's worth giving it a shot. The rewards could be delicious.

Chilies love heat, so they do best in warm and/or tropical environments. They also love humidity. So if you live in the tropics or the desert, you're in luck. Your chilies should have no problem growing and thriving. If you do not live in a tropical climate, don't abandon all hope. As long as you live somewhere that has a decent summer, you should still be able to raise some chili plants. You can also extend the growing season by growing them indoors or in a greenhouse.

The most important thing you should consider, of course, is what sort of chilies you like best and are most likely to eat and enjoy. There's little sense in growing habanero peppers, cute and orange as they are, if you aren't a fan of their searing heat. Take time to consider if you like hot, mild, or medium chilies, and which ones are the most visually appealing to you. Nearly all chilies make lovely, brightly hued ornamental plants, but chilies like New Mexico and Anaheim also produce big, glossy green leaves.

For beginner growers who are just getting started, the shorter growing time of the capsicum annuum species makes it the best option. These peppers will also fare better in cooler climates. Luckily, the most common and popular chili varieties—jalapeños, serranos, poblanos, Anaheims, cayenne, and pasillas—belong to this "annual" species. So wherever you live, you're likely to have better luck with these peppers.

FACT

The most popular chili plants to grow—and the ones most often found at nurseries—include the jalapeño, banana, Hungarian wax, poblano, serrano, and habanero peppers. But don't let that stop you from seeking out other types of peppers from smaller growers or specialty seed stores. Why not try a Bolivian Rainbow, Devil's Tongue, white habanero, or a Bishop's Crown?

Chili plants will grow into small to medium-sized bushes from one-and-a-half to three-feet tall. Exactly how big they get depends on the species and variety, but you'll want to make sure, whether you're growing them indoors in pots or outside in a plot, that they have enough room to spread their leaves.

Here are some quick tips for growing your pepper plants:

▼   **QUICK TIPS FOR GROWING PEPPERS**

Family name	Solanaceae (Nightshade family)
Edible parts	Fruits
Location	Very sunny area
Best Soil	Fertile, well-drained soil that does not have an excess of nitrogen; soil that is too rich will form leaves but poor fruiting; pH 5.5–6.8.
When to plant	Sow seeds indoors 6 to 8 weeks before you plan to put them into your garden. Transplant them when the temperature is 65°F.
How to plant	Set out plants 18 inches apart in rows spaced 30 to 36 inches apart.
How much to plant	5 to 10 plants per person.
Companion plants	Plant with basil, carrots, onions, oregano, and marjoram. Fennel will have a negative effect on peppers, so avoid planting them near each other.
Weeding	Keep well weeded when plants are small.
Watering	Water regularly and keep soil moist when the plant is flowering and fruiting.
Fertilizing	Use fish fertilizer or compost tea after the first bloom and then after the fruit starts to form.
Pests and diseases	Aphids, armyworms, Colorado potato beetles, corn borers, mites, and cutworms are some common pests.
When to harvest	Peppers mature between 60 and 95 days after planting depending on the variety. Harvest hot peppers when they are full size and have turned yellow, red, or dark green depending on the variety.
How to harvest	Cut or gently pull the pepper from the plant, leaving a stem of ½ inch.
Storage	Fresh peppers will last 1 to 2 weeks in the refrigerator if not washed and placed in a sealed plastic bag. Peppers can be frozen, dried, and preserved by pickling or canning them.

Growing from Seed

There are plenty of technicalities and rules and suggestions for growing your own chilies from seed. Just a few minutes of research, both online and in gardening books, can leave you pretty overwhelmed by the amount of information out there, especially if you have never done it before. Julian Livsey at The Chile Man, *www.thechileman.org,* has written a great, concise guide for absolute beginners. Drawing from Livsey's expertise, consider the following a simple, straightforward guide for beginners. (For more detailed growing tips, consult gardening books.) For now, don't be intimidated, just dig in and get started.

First, you'll need some seeds. There are a seemingly endless variety of chilies to choose from, so novices would do well to stick with some of the capsicum annuums mentioned in this chapter because they are a bit easier to grow. (If you have your heart set on a particular variety, though, do as the chilies do: Be bold and go for it.) You can get seeds at a local gardening store, online, or, if you prefer, just buy some peppers at the store and scrape the seeds out from the inside.

QUESTION

Where can I buy chili seeds online?
Some good online seed resources include: Reimer Seeds, *www* *.reimerseeds.com*; Rainbow Chili Seeds, *www.rainbowchiliseeds.com*; Terra Time & Tide, *www.pepperhot.com*; Peppermania, *www* *.bayoutraders.com*.

Germinating Seeds

Once you've got your seeds, the next move is to turn them into plants. First goal: germination, which requires heat, moisture, and oxygen. The best way to do this is in soil, though you could also do it in materials like paper towels or wool. You don't need anything fancy to hold your soil—planting cells will work great or even just a simple plastic box with some drainage holes poked into the bottom.

Put a little soil in the bottom of your container, then sow your seeds on the surface of the soil. Cover them with just enough soil so they are just below the surface. If you plant them too deep, you will effectively be burying your seeds alive. They will run out of energy before they ever reach the surface of the soil. So give them a fighting chance and keep them close to the surface.

For moisture, water the surface of the soil. You want the soil to be moist, but not watery. Just a little bit of water should do. For heat, place the container in a reasonably warm place—above a radiator, on a sunny windowsill. Just be sure to keep an eye on it. If the container gets too hot, the moisture will evaporate from the soil and the seeds will go dormant.

Depending upon the variety that you are growing, your seeds will take anywhere from a few days to several weeks to break the surface. Your patience will eventually be rewarded when you see them break through the surface. Hurrah, seedlings! They now need plenty of light, so move them to a sunny window or a greenhouse, if you are able. At this stage, the seedlings are also very delicate, so resist the urge to touch, poke, or pet them.

Transplanting

Chili plants tend to produce leaves in pairs. The first set are called the seed leaves, and they are preview leaves of sorts. The next set that develops will be the first real leaves. Once your seedlings have these, you will need to move them to a larger pot to give them more room to grow. Start with a pot that is at least 4"–6" wide, then move up to bigger pots as necessary, or when you see the roots starting to peek through the drainage holes. (Important: only use pots that have drainage holes on the bottom.) If you leave them in a small pot, it will inhibit the full growth of the plant, which might be your goal if you are in a little apartment. Be sure to handle the plants gently and carefully when transplanting, as chilies really hate having their roots disturbed.

ESSENTIAL

Transplant your vegetables on a cloudy day or later in the day when the sun is not so hot. The hot sun can wilt or scorch the young leaves, leaving them stressed. Make sure the transplants are moist before you plant them and gently water them after they have been placed in the ground. Watering the plant will help the roots become established.

Kitchen/Container Gardening

Those of you in the city with studio apartments or tiny fire escape balconies will be pleased to know that you can also grow chili pepper plants. Chilies (again, the capsicum annuums in particular) are good container plants if they live in pots that are large enough to hold them. A big pot is not a problem, but one that is too small is. Although many peppers don't grow to more than a foot-and-a-half or so tall, they still need enough room for their roots to spread out.

For smaller peppers (under 12" tall), a 2 gallon container will suffice. For the larger pepper plants, a 5 gallon or even 10 gallon container will give the peppers plenty of room to grow. Again, be sure your container has drainage holes, so excess water has a way to escape.

The Advantages of Container Gardening

One of the great advantages to growing in containers is they take up very little space. Containers can be placed on a balcony, porch, or patio; they can sit on a windowsill, attach to balcony railings, or hang in baskets from the rafters. They can also be used in your backyard to grow veggies that may not do well in your soil or to enhance a spot in your existing garden. Whatever option you choose, containers will provide you with some great vegetables to enjoy. Container gardens also take less time to maintain than a backyard garden. You'll spend much less time weeding your vegetables if you grow them in containers because the pepper plant usually fills the pot, leaving less room for the weeds to grow. Growing in containers can save you a sore back. Bending, lifting, digging, and twisting are all regular activities for a bed gardener. Gardeners with physical disabilities or back problems often find it difficult to garden. Using containers is one way to make it easier to grow peppers. Choose containers that are the height that works for you or place smaller containers on a table or bench to make them easier to reach and enjoy. Growing peppers in containers can add a decorative touch to your garden or patio. The containers themselves can be very attractive and because your pepper plants will produce fruits that are green, red, yellow, and orange, the plants themselves can add color, texture, and interest to a dull or somewhat boring space.

Heat-loving vegetables such as peppers are often more productive when grown in containers because the soil heats up more quickly and stays warmer. This is especially important if you live in a cool, damp climate or have unpredictable summer temperatures. These types of vegetables often need shelter from the wind and rain as well, so growing them in a container allows you the freedom to easily move them to a more sheltered area when necessary.

Disadvantages to Container Growing

Your backyard garden often only needs watering once or twice a week because the plant roots can pull water from deep in the soil, but plants that are grown in containers do not have this option. Most containers need watering every day, but some need attention twice a day, especially during the summer months or in a hot climate. Because containers need watering so often, it is difficult to leave them unattended for any length of time. Purchasing containers and the soil needed to fill them can also be expensive. The cost will depend on how many containers you need, the sizes, and the type of containers you choose to purchase. If you are planning to grow your peppers in a container for several years, choose a good quality one so it will last. Containers need to be cleaned on a regular basis to keep them free of pests and diseases, so choose a container that is easy to take care of. In a garden bed you use the existing soil that is there, but in a container you need to purchase the soil. Some or all of the soil needs to be replenished every year since the vegetable plants will use all the nutrients.

ESSENTIAL

Making a shopping list before you even enter the garden center will save you time and money. Before you go, decide which varieties of peppers you want to grow, where you will put the containers, how many containers you will need, and what sizes you need to grow your plants.

Even though there are a few disadvantages to growing your vegetables in containers, it is definitely worth growing this way, especially if you only have a small space to grow in. Be creative!

The Container

When choosing a container for your plants, there are three important rules to remember: first, the container must be deep enough to hold enough soil to accommodate the plant's root growth; second, it must be large enough for the plant to grow to maturity; and finally, water must be able to drain easily from the bottom of the container so the soil does not get waterlogged. The container can be any shape so long as it can fulfill these three essentials. Vegetables such as peppers need a container more than sixteen inches wide and at least eighteen inches deep to grow well. For best results, use transplants when growing these vegetables. Grow only one plant in each container. You could even grow vegetables with shallow roots such as lettuce or salad greens around the base of your pepper plants once they are established. There are many options for large garden pots at your garden center, but they can be expensive to purchase. Instead, reuse garbage cans, wooden barrels, metal washbasins, or old wheelbarrows.

When making a decision on what kind of container you want, take into account your climate and whether you will be leaving your containers outside all year long. In cold climates, the soil in your containers may freeze, which can split or break your container. If you get a lot of strong winds, lightweight containers can be blown around and damaged. If you choose not to grow anything in your containers during the off season, make sure you put them in a sheltered area such as a garage or shed so they will be protected. If you are growing your peppers all year long, it is important that the soil does not get too waterlogged and the container is protected if you get a cold spell.

Container Soil

Soil is probably the most important aspect of growing great peppers in containers. The soil holds all the nutrients and retains all the moisture your plants need to grow. The soil needs to be rich but still lightweight enough so you can easily move your containers around. There are some excellent commercial soil mixes specifically made for container growing. Peat moss, vermiculite, and perlite make them lighter and well-rotted manures or compost keeps them from drying out too quickly. These commercial mixes are sterile, which means they are free of any soil-borne diseases and they have the basic elements of nitrogen, potassium, and phosphorous. You can make your own soil mix; just remember not to use your regular garden soil, because it is too heavy for containers and will become compacted. All container soils need to be light enough to allow good air circulation for the vegetable plants to get oxygen.

Here is a simple recipe for making your own container soil. All ingredients can easily be bought at your local garden center. Simply mix the following ingredients together:

- One cubic foot of peat moss
- One cubic foot of vermiculite
- Six ounces of lime
- Six ounces of bone meal
- One ounce of blood or alfalfa meal
- One ounce of langbeinite

One cubic foot is twelve inches in length, twelve inches in width, and twelve inches deep.

Before planting your containers, make sure the soil is well watered. The commercial soil mixes or your homemade container soil will absorb warm water more easily. When first seeding your containers, make sure they are kept in a fairly warm area but not in the direct sunlight. This will allow the seed to germinate without drying out too quickly. Seeds need to be moist in order to germinate and young transplants need more water so their shallow roots can reach the moisture. This means watering your containers often— at least once a day, sometimes twice.

Watering and Fertilizing

The biggest disadvantage to growing your vegetables in containers is the amount of watering they need. The size of the container, the vegetables you are growing, and the weather all determine how often and how much you need to water. When your vegetable plants are young, they need to be watered more often because the soil dries out from the top down; since your young plants do not have a deep root system yet, they need more water nearer the top of the container. As your vegetable plants mature, the roots go deeper and therefore need less frequent watering.

How Much Water?

To see whether your container needs to be watered, stick your index finger into the soil up to the knuckle. If you can feel moisture, do not water. If the soil feels dry, give the container a good drink. The container has had enough water if you can feel the moisture two to three inches from the top after you've let it sit for a few minutes. If the container is quite dry, the water will drain quickly from the bottom, leaving very little water for the soil to absorb. If this is the case, keep giving the container a drink every few minutes until the water stops draining from the bottom.

Overwatering is as big of a problem as underwatering, so make sure you check your containers regularly—as much as twice a day if the pots are small and it is a hot day. Use mulch to help keep the moisture from evaporating from your container. Mulching the top of the soil with moss, leaves, grass clippings, or even shredded newspaper can prevent the moisture from evaporating too quickly, especially in hot weather. Mulching also works well when you are growing vegetable plants that prefer a cooler soil because it will keep the soil a bit cooler as well.

If you are going away on vacation, especially for an extended period during the summer months, make sure you have someone water your containers while you are gone. Using a drip system on a timer is an option if you are going to be gone for a short period of time; just make sure the hoses are secured in the containers so they get watered properly. If you only have a few pots, cut off the bottom of a soda bottle or plastic milk carton, place the top of the bottle securely into the soil, and then fill the container with water. If the container is well moistened to begin with, the water will slowly be released as it is needed. This is a great option if you are gone for only a day or two. Do not use a sprinkler when watering your containers because the container may not get enough water.

Fertilizing

Moisture is important for growing your vegetables, but so are nutrients. Plants that are grown in containers have a limited supply of soil and therefore a limited supply of nutrients. To make sure your plants produce great fruit and pods, fertilize the soil. Gardeners often think that buying a good commercial soil mix will be enough to sustain the needs of their vegetable plants all season, but plants need a little boost during the season.

FACT

Another option for apartment gardening when you are tight on space is a hydroponic "windowfarm" system. The website *www.windowfarms.org* sells kits that allow you to grow plants in plastic water bottles in a hanging system right in your window. The hydroponic kit, which contains an air pump and plastic tubing, delivers nutrient-rich water straight to the roots of chili pepper plants. Sounds a little complicated, but it's actually quite simple and allows you to grow quite a few plants without taking up counter or table space.

Taking Care of Your Chili Pepper Plant

You may want to consider feeding your chili plants a little fertilizer. But fertilizer is far from absolutely necessary. The right balance of light and water is really all that the plant needs (easier said than done, yes, but it's true). Keep a close eye on your plant and as long as your soil is halfway decent, the plant will be able to get all the nutrients it needs from that.

Most fertilizer mixes that you can buy come with a mix of NPK, which is nitrogen, phosphorus, potassium. Too much nitrogen and your plants will be all leaves and no fruit, so be judicious in your fertilizer use.

When your chili plants begin producing flowers that means you are really cooking with gas. From the flower comes the fruit. Here is the simplest method for pollinating your flowers: When there are several flowers open on your plant, rub your finger around the middle part to pick up the pollen, and repeat a couple of times for each flower. This will move the pollen to the stamen and start the chemical reaction needed to make the fruit.

ALERT

To increase the chili yield of your plants, try harvesting green fruits before they are fully ripe. The number of chili pods produced by a chili plant will, at one, reach a maximum. Therefore, to increase the yield during what might be your plant's most productive season, keep harvesting the fruits before they ripen fully and drop to the ground. This stimulates flowering and fruiting.

If everything goes well, the flower's petals will drop off as the green middle part of the flower starts to swell. This is the chili pepper beginning to grow. Keep your plant happy and produce fruit for a few months.

A couple things to keep in mind: Be sure to plant sweet peppers and chili peppers in separate pots and areas of the garden. Peppers have a predilection for cross-pollinating if they are grown in close proximity to each other. So a jalapeño will gladly get friendly with a habanero or a bell pepper. It could be fascinating, but if you serve your guest a stuffed bell pepper that's as spicy as a serrano, the fun will be over fast.

What to Do with Chili Pepper Leaves

The fruit of the chili plant might get all the attention, but don't overlook those lovely green leaves. Like radish and turnip tops and broccoli stems, chili leaves are too often discarded. While most people don't think to eat them, they are completely edible—not to mention tasty. As long as you're going to the trouble of nurturing and tending to your precious chili plant, you may as well use and enjoy as much of it as possible.

In Western cultures and cuisine, chili leaves are easily forgotten. However, in Asian cuisines they are a staple. One of the national dishes of the Philippines, *tinola*, is a light soup made with chicken broth, ginger, chayote squash, and chili leaves, which give the dish a distinct aroma and flavor. In Korea, chili leaves are often used in the country's iconic kimchi, preserved and fermented right along with cabbage. The Japanese also like to cook chili leaves, most often "tsukudani" style—simmered in soy sauce and mirin. They also sauté the greens simply.

Chili leaves have a distinct bite and pungency, but they are not nearly as spicy as the peppers with which they grow. Some describe the flavor as slightly bitter, but they are akin to spinach, just with a little more earthiness and depth of flavor. You can substitute chili leaves for spinach in recipes, or simply sauté it like any other green such as chard or kale. Just be sure to cook it thoroughly so as to reduce its bite.

CHAPTER 5

Chilies in the Kitchen: Handling and Prep

As you've seen, chili peppers, with their vibrant colors and flavors, have influenced many of the world's cuisines. They are integral to how people around the globe eat now. It's time to put stories and ideas away and get to work with chilies in your own kitchen. These pungent fruits enliven all kinds of dishes and are among the most fun ingredients to use, as long you understand how to handle them properly and safely.

How to Handle Chilies Safely

You can't see or taste capsaicin (the substance that gives chili peppers their fire), but your mouth, eyes, nose, and skin certainly can. It's a serious irritant, and one that increases with a pepper's spiciness. Many people have a hard time handling chilies with their bare hands, as the capsaicin turns their hands red, makes them sting, and sometimes even produces blisters. For this reason, when handling chilies in the kitchen and prepping them for cooking, it's a good idea to put on a pair of rubber gloves. The thin barrier of rubber will go a long way in saving you pain and discomfort while cutting, chopping, and deseeding the peppers. But be careful, of course, not to touch your eyes or nose or any other sensitive areas with your gloved hands.

When working with a fairly milder chili (such as Hungarian wax peppers or poblanos), going glove-free is less risky. But even though there's less capsaicin and less likelihood of burns and irritation, always use caution—especially when handling the seeds and white ribs found inside. Likewise, if you prefer not to don gloves at all, be extremely cautious and remember to wash your hands thoroughly with soap and water after you are done handling the peppers. For those who intend to go gloveless, another idea is to handle the hot peppers under running water. By doing this, some of the capsaicin will immediately be washed away instead of having the time to seep into your skin and scald you.

There is also less to worry about when handling dried chili peppers. Since most of the water has evaporated from the fruit, there's no risk of fresh juices squirting out and flying onto skin or eyes. However, capsaicin oils are still present, so be careful and, again, be sure to rinse your hands off after you are done handling the dried chilies.

ALERT

When grinding dried chilies, you need to be aware of the chili dust that can be let loose into the air. Those little bits of chili can irritate your eyes as well as your nose and throat if they are inhaled. Try to work with them in a well-ventilated area. And while you don't need to don a surgical mask, make sure to turn away before taking any deep breaths.

How to Chop, Slice, and Dice Chilies

Capsaicin, and its fiery and potentially harmful power, lies inside a chili's seeds and white ribs. Many recipes call for peppers to be *seeded*, which means removing these chemically loaded parts. Removing them removes much of the heat, but whether you are wearing rubber gloves or not, oils from the pepper will be released into the air and onto your cutting board and knife, creating potential sources of irritation. Just like onions, the scent of chili peppers can also bother the eyes and nose, so make sure you're in a ventilated area and/or can take fresh breaths of air.

As with all fresh fruits and vegetables, give your chili peppers a good rinse under the faucet to clean off any dirt or grime. Then, to seed them, slice the pepper in half lengthwise, from the stem end to the tip. If you're comfortable with the knife and have a steady hand, slice through sideways, down and away from you, rather than just slicing down and into the pepper. (This method reduces the risk of chili juices splashing up into your face.) Using care, slice out the white ribs, veins, and seeds with the tip of your knife. If you're feeling crafty, you could also hold the pepper by the stem and scrape downward using a melon baller, which will make it easier to scrape all the insides away in one fell swoop. Discard the toxic insides.

QUESTION

Do you always have to seed chili peppers?
Even if a recipe instructs you to seed chili peppers, feel free to ignore the directive. Recipes aren't laws you must obey; they are guidelines for you to follow. Trust your own tastes. If you want the full heat of a serrano, leave its insides intact. If you want moderate heat, seed just one half of the pepper, or remove the seeds and leave the ribs. It's up to you.

If your recipe calls for *sliced peppers*, cut the seeded pepper halves lengthwise into strips of your desired width. If it calls for *diced pepper*, group the strips together on cutting board, position them horizontally, then cut crosswise to the desired size.

How to Deal with Chili Burns

Even if you are careful, it's still quite easy to end up with a capsaicin burn. Just wiping down a pepper-ridden cutting board, or touching a stray seed here and there can bother the skin. It happens to everyone. First step, if the burn is on your hands and fingers, avoid getting them anywhere near your mouth or eyes. Next, wash your hands with some vegetable oil and warm water. Capsaicin is not water soluble, but it is oil soluble, so the oil will help lift the capsaicin from the surface of your skin. The water will help whisk it all down the drain.

Chili Burns inside the Mouth

When you eat chili peppers, capsaicin run wilds in your mouth, creating that fiery sensation that will cause you pain, pleasure and, possibly, perspiration. If the heat becomes too much to bear, know that it will eventually subside. Unfortunately, there is no surefire "cure" for a chili burn besides time. But there are a few well-proven tactics to reduce the amount of pain you're in. Calm down; drink a glass of cold milk. If you've got yogurt on hand, have a few spoonfuls. You can also spread butter on a slice of bread and eat that. The fats and oils in these dairy products will absorb good amounts of the capsaicin that is burning your mouth off.

QUESTION

Will eating starchy foods cure the chili burn?
No, eating starchy foods like white bread, pasta, or white rice will not immediately extinguish the four-alarm chili pepper fire that's raging in your mouth. But eaten alongside spicy dishes, these starches do help. It's no accident that white rice accompanies so many spicy Asian dishes like curries and Szechuan stir-fries: the grains soak up extra capsaicin that could be scorching your tongue, tempering the oral inferno.

Again, capsaicin is not water soluble, so drinking water won't help that much—especially if you gargle or slosh the water around in your mouth. If you do either, all you'll succeed in doing is spreading waves of capsaicin throughout your mouth, triggering more pain, doing more harm than good. A quick, big, no-nonsense glug of water straight down the gullet will give a feeling of temporary relief, though, so go ahead and down the H_2O. A cold beer or two might also help, mostly because alcohol carries the added bonus of relaxing and numbing your mind and body.

It's worth noting here that capsaicin is not broken down by the digestive system. So, while you might succeed in cooling down your mouth, just remember what goes in must also go out. It's a sensitive subject, but consider yourself warned: if you eat spicy food, be prepared for it to leave your system via what many chili-heads have dubbed the "ring of fire."

FACT

It seems every culture has its own recommended method for curing a chili burn. While they may not be scientifically proven, locals in Thailand, Mexico, and other countries swear by these remedies: taking a bite of fresh cucumber, touching the affected area with corn tortillas, eating honey, munching a raw carrot, and sucking on a fresh lemon or lime. These tactics may or may not work, but in the heat of the moment, they just might be worth a shot.

Storing Chilies

The best place for storing fresh chilies is in the refrigerator or tucked away in a cool, dark cupboard. Storing chilies in plastic bags will trap moisture and cause them to rot at a quicker pace, so keeping them in a brown paper bag or wrapped in paper towels is preferred. Chili peppers stored in either of these manners should keep in the refrigerator for about a week. Peppers continue to ripen after they are picked, so unless you want to speed up the process, keep them away from other fruits like apples or bananas.

If you find yourself with more chilies than you have time to make good use of, you can easily preserve them for later use. Because capsaicin retains its heat for long periods under harsh conditions, chili peppers make good candidates for freezing. The quickest way to do this is by cutting them in half, removing excess seeds, and slicing them into thin pieces. Blanch them in boiling water for a few minutes, then plunge them in an ice bath for an equal amount of time. Drain them thoroughly, then place in an airtight container or zip-top bag and put them in the freezer. When you're ready to use them, simply thaw and add them to soups or stews when they are bubbling away on the stove. It's best to use these peppers for flavor in hot, long-simmering dishes instead of in salads or stir-fries since this process rids them of the crispiness and snap that are characteristic of fresh chilies.

Drying Chilies

Chilies can also be dried for long-term storage and use down the road. The easiest and safest way to do this is in the oven. Place your chilies on a wire rack (either straight in the oven or on a wire rack set onto a cookie or baking sheet) and set your oven to its lowest setting, between 100°F–150°F. Remember, the goal is to dry the chilies, not cook them, so keep the temperature as low as possible and keep an eye on how things are progressing. The process should take between six to ten hours, depending on pepper size. Be sure to flip them every three hours for even drying. To speed the whole process up, you can slice your chilies in half or into thin rings and arrange them on a lined baking tray.

Air Drying

If you can't be bothered to stay at home for a day and monitor the slow progress of your oven, you might consider air drying your chilies. This method works best in a screened-in porch or similarly protected area with lots of air circulation. Take firm, ripe red chilies that still have their stems, then tie the stems to a sturdy piece of twine, giving each chili a few inches of space from its neighbor. Hang the line of chilies (you can think of it as something akin to a clothesline) in a dry area that gets plenty of air.

Chilies are blessed with very elastic and watertight skin, so it may as long as a few weeks for your peppers to thoroughly dry out. You might poke a few holes in them to speed up the process. Over time, the chilies' bright red skin will transform to deep, shiny red. Their skins will be crinkled and dry, but still feel smooth.

How do you make a *ristra*, a string of hanging chilies?
Ristras are a traditional Mexican method for drying chili bunches. Both practical and visually appealing, ristras became popular and are now standard décor in households and restaurants in the Southwest United States and beyond. To make a ristra, take ripe red peppers, make a small slit on each side of the pepper just below the stem, then run a needle and thread through the slits to string the peppers together. Use waxed thread or dental floss as the capsaicin from chilies will dissolve ordinary string. Hang in a warm, dry place.

Sun Drying

Sun drying is not an option for everyone because it requires warm temperatures, low humidity, and a near constant breeze. This method really only works in arid areas like New Mexico (where chilies are famously dried on rooftops), and is not advised for most people. After several days of direct sunlight and no precipitation, the chilies will be dry enough for sunlight to shine through their skins. If you successfully sun dry chilies, you'll need to decontaminate them from insects (not to mention their eggs) that may have crept inside. You can freeze the chilies or set them in a 200°F oven for half an hour to do so.

Rehydrating Chilies

To revive your chilies from their dried slumber and back into a usable state, wash them gently under the kitchen tap and put a small pot of water to boil on the stove. Place the chilies in a bowl, then pour in the hot water until they are just covered. Let the chilies soak for at least fifteen minutes (longer if they are especially tough). The longer they soak, the softer they'll become and the easier they'll be to slice, chop, or blend.

ALERT

Don't throw away that chili-soaking water! In fact, don't even think about throwing away that soaking water. It is loaded with spicy chili goodness that can add a punch to multiple dishes. You can use it to thin-out cooked sauces like adobo or mole, or you can pour it into a jar or Tupperware and keep it in the refrigerator for later use. When you're making chili or soup, add some of this liquid to the broth for more flavor.

If you have a little extra time, consider drying off your chilies and then roasting/toasting them lightly on a comal (a smooth, flat griddle) or in a cast iron pan. This will help release their oils (not to mention some wonderful aromas) and awaken their flavors. Be careful not to burn the chilies, or else their flavor will quickly turn bitter. A minute or so on the hot stove should suffice.

CHAPTER 6

Making Your Own: Homemade Hot Sauces

⅔ cup dried red chili flakes

⅓ cup Chinese fermented black beans, roughly chopped

4 large cloves garlic, peeled and lightly smashed

2 tablespoons fresh ginger root, peeled and finely minced

2½ cups peanut oil

⅓ cup sesame oil

Chinese Chili Oil

This easy-to-assemble chili oil is a great hot sauce to have on hand in your kitchen. Drizzle it into stir fries, rice, and soup. When you use it, make sure to scoop some of those flavorful bits that settle on the bottom.

1. Combine all ingredients in a heavy, non-aluminum saucepan. Rest a thermometer on the rim of the pot. Bring the mixture to a bubble over low-to-medium heat (between 225°–250°F) stirring occasionally. Let it simmer 15 minutes, making sure the temperature doesn't rise.

2. Remove from the heat and let stand until cool.

3. Pour the oil and solids into a clean glass jar. Cover and store in the refrigerator. Take it out of the fridge and let it come to room temperature before using.

What Are Chinese Black Beans?

Chinese black beans are nothing like the black beans you'll find in burritos or Mexican restaurants. These fermented black beans (also called salted or dried black beans) are actually soybeans that have been dried and fermented with salt. They have a pungent, salty flavor and are used throughout Chinese cooking.

½ cup mayonnaise

½ cup sour cream

2 cans chipotle chilies, finely chopped

Pinch of dried oregano leaves

Chipotle Mayo

This spicy mayo makes a great addition to sandwiches and burgers. You can easily double or triple this recipe, and feel free to use low-fat mayo or sour cream.

1. In a medium bowl, combine the mayonnaise and sour cream.

2. Add the chopped chilies, along with a bit of the sauce from the can, and the oregano.

3. Stir all the ingredients until well blended.

4. Cover and refrigerate. Let it chill for at least an hour before use so the flavors can come together.

2 ounces (about 15–20) dried hot red chili peppers, stems and seeds removed

4 cloves garlic, peeled

1 teaspoon ground caraway

1 teaspoon ground coriander

½ teaspoon salt

2–4 tablespoons olive oil

Harissa

Harissa is a Tunisian hot sauce that is used throughout North African cooking. Extra spices give it a great flavor that is much more than simply spicy. Harissa adds a welcome boost to cooked lentils, beans, and soups.

1. Soak the chili peppers in hot water for 15 minutes, or until they are nice and soft.

2. Drain the peppers, then combine with garlic, spices, and salt in a food processor.

3. Blend the ingredients, adding a little bit of olive oil, to make a paste.

4. Pour into a clean glass jar and cover with a little oil. Refrigerated, it will keep for a few weeks.

Grinding Spices

You can buy ground spices at the supermarket, but consider buying them whole and grinding them as needed. It only takes a few seconds to grind them (you can use an electric coffee grinder or do it by hand with a mortar and pestle) and you'll notice that the flavors are stronger and brighter.

1 bunch of cilantro, stems included

3–6 serrano peppers, depending on your preference, seeded (if you like it very spicy, feel free to leave the ribs and seeds in)

6 garlic cloves, peeled and roughly chopped (resist the urge to use less)

½ teaspoon ground cumin

Salt, to taste

Olive oil

Lemon juice, to taste

Zhug

Zhug is a downright fiery sauce that is eaten daily in Yemen, where it's believed to keep away illness. One taste of its potent garlic flavor and you'll understand why. A little zhug goes a long way on sandwiches, as well as roasted or grilled chicken and fish.

1. Wash the cilantro well and pat dry. Coarsely chop leaves and stems. Place in a food processor.

2. Add the chopped serranos, garlic, cumin, and salt to the food processor.

3. Blend. Add enough olive oil to make a rough paste.

4. Taste and adjust seasoning to your liking. Add lemon juice if you like.

5. Place in a clean jar. Refrigerated, this will keep for a few weeks.

¼ teaspoon whole allspice

¼ teaspoon black peppercorns

¼ teaspoon cumin seeds

1 pint tequila blanco

5 fresh red Thai chilies, lightly smashed with the side of a knife (you could also use dried chilies)

Tequila Hot Sauce

This simple, boozy sauce is especially delicious on grilled fish. This sauce will become more flavorful the longer it sits. Also, the higher quality the tequila you use, the better the sauce will be.

1. Toast allspice, peppercorns, and cumin in a skillet over medium eat until they are fragrant, about 2–3 minutes. Remove from heat and set aside.

2. Unscrew the tequila bottle and take a shot or two (or just pour out about 1" worth from the bottle) to make room for other ingredients.

3. Add the spices and chilies to the tequila bottle.

4. Screw the top back on (or add a pour spot). Let sauce sit for one week before using.

Different Types of Tequila

Tequila blanco, or "white tequila," is un-aged and immediately bottled after distillation. It tastes cleaner and a bit harsher than other types of tequilas. Tequila *reposado* ("rested") is aged in oak barrels for at least two months, while *añejo* ("aged") stays in oak barrels for at least one year. These tequilas are smoother and more complex tasting.

INGREDIENTS | MAKES ABOUT 2 CUPS

3 tablespoons vegetable oil

1 medium onion, finely minced

½ cup celery, finely chopped

4 garlic cloves, peeled and minced

¾ cup apple cider vinegar

½ cup tomato paste

½ cup water

2 tablespoons molasses

3 tablespoons light brown sugar

2 tablespoons Worcestershire sauce

2 teaspoons hot paprika

1 teaspoon powdered mustard

½ teaspoon ground black pepper

½ teaspoon cayenne pepper

1 tablespoon kosher salt

Kansas City–Style Barbecue Sauce

A classic, all-purpose barbecue sauce to use on all kinds of meats. Slather this onto grilled meats, paint it on meat during the last few minutes of cooking, or use it as a dipping sauce on your plate. For extra spice, add more cayenne.

1. In heavy saucepan, heat the vegetable oil over medium heat. Add the onion, celery, and garlic, and cook until softened, about 5 minutes.

2. Add the rest of the ingredients and simmer the sauce, uncovered, for 30 minutes, stirring occasionally. The sauce should be quite thick.

3. Purée the sauce in a blender until smooth.

4. Store in an airtight container in the refrigerator, where it will keep for a couple of weeks.

INGREDIENTS | MAKES ABOUT 3 CUPS

¼ cup vegetable oil

2 large onions, minced

¼ cup celery, finely chopped

4 garlic cloves, peeled and minced

½ cup apple cider vinegar

¼ cup distilled white vinegar

¾ cup ketchup

½ cup tomato sauce

½ cup water

2 tablespoons Worcestershire sauce

1 tablespoon chili powder

1½ teaspoons ground cumin

1 teaspoon hot paprika

1 tablespoon coarse salt

Texas-Style Barbecue Sauce

This barbecue sauce is thinner and less sweet than the Kansas City–Style Barbecue Sauce, but it's also got the added bonus of the flavor and spices of the Southwest. Feel free to turn up the heat with a little extra chili powder.

1. In a heavy saucepan, heat the vegetable oil over medium heat. Add the onion, celery, and garlic, and cook until softened, about 5 minutes.

2. Add all the remaining ingredients and simmer the sauce, uncovered and stirring occasionally, for 20 minutes. It should be quite thick.

3. Purée the sauce in a blender until smooth.

4. Store in an airtight container in the refrigerator, where it will keep for a couple of weeks.

Different Styles of Barbecue

Barbecue is a highly contentious matter for many Americans, especially in the south. What Texans think of as barbecue is nothing like what people from North Carolina picture (to say nothing of the difference between Western and Eastern Carolina barbecue). Carolina sauces are generally more vinegar-y than Texas and Kansas City sauces. One thing everyone agrees on: Whatever the style, barbecue sauce makes meat even more delicious.

1 (28-ounce) can of whole tomatoes

2 tablespoons olive oil

1 medium onion, finely chopped

1 tablespoon tomato paste

⅓ cup packed dark brown sugar

¼ cup apple cider vinegar

½ teaspoon salt

½ teaspoon crushed red pepper flakes

¼ teaspoon ground cayenne pepper

½ teaspoon ground cumin

Spicy Ketchup

It may seem crazy at first to make your own ketchup, but homemade ketchup is much better tasting and far less sweet than the bottled stuff. (It's also better for you because it's not loaded with high fructose corn syrup.) Think ketchup, but with a spicy twist. Use it on the usual suspects—burgers, French fries, and eggs.

1. Purée the canned whole tomatoes (along with their juices) in a blender until smooth.

2. In a heavy saucepan heat the oil over medium heat and cook the onion until softened, about 5 minutes.

3. Add the puréed tomatoes and rest of the ingredients and simmer, uncovered and stirring occasionally, until the mixture is quite thick, about an hour.

4. Purée the ketchup in batches in a blender until smooth. Cover the top of the blender with a towel and be careful when blending hot liquids, as they will expand.

5. Transfer the ketchup to a clean, airtight container. Let chill for at least 2 hours before using. Store in the refrigerator.

8–10 red bird's-eye chilies, seeds and ribs removed, chopped

6 tablespoons fresh lime juice

4 teaspoons dark brown sugar

1 tablespoon olive oil

1 tablespoon fresh ginger, finely chopped

½ tablespoon white vinegar

½ teaspoon kosher salt

2 cloves garlic, peeled and roughly chopped

Piri Piri Sauce

Piri piri is the Swahili term for hot chili. It's also the name of Mozambique's national dish. Throughout the country, this sauce is found on most tables, where it's added to fish and chicken dishes. It makes a great dipping sauce for shrimp and also makes a nice addition to eggs and steak.

1. In a blender, combine all the ingredients and purée into a chunky sauce.

2. Transfer to a clean jar and store in the refrigerator for up to 1 week.

1 stalk lemongrass, outer leaves removed and discarded, inner core finely chopped

2 green chilies (you can use Thai chilies or jalapeños), roughly chopped

1 shallot, roughly chopped

4 cloves of garlic, peeled and roughly chopped

1 thumb-sized piece of ginger, peeled and thinly sliced

1 bunch cilantro, stems included, roughly chopped

½ cup fresh basil

½ teaspoon ground cumin

3 tablespoons fish sauce

1 teaspoon shrimp paste (optional)

2 tablespoons lime juice

1 teaspoon brown sugar

3 tablespoons coconut milk, or enough to help blend ingredients together and make paste

Green Curry Paste

Sure, you can buy green curry paste, but making it from scratch is not only easy, it will make your kitchen smell incredible. You'll probably need to open a can of coconut milk to make this, so use the rest of its contents to make a curry for dinner.

1. Place all the ingredients in a food processor or blender.

2. Purée into a smooth paste, adding a little more coconut milk if necessary.

3. Taste and adjust seasoning. If it's too salty, add more lime juice. Add extra chili for more spice.

4. Place in an airtight container. In the refrigerator, it will keep for about 1 week.

3 tablespoons coriander seeds, toasted

2 teaspoons cumin seeds, toasted

6–8 red serrano chilies, seeded and chopped

1 medium onion, chopped

2 garlic cloves, chopped

1 stalk lemongrass, outer leaves removed and discarded, inner core finely chopped

1 thumb-sized piece of ginger, finely chopped

2 tablespoons lime juice

2 teaspoons hot paprika

2 tablespoons tamarind concentrate

3 tablespoons fish sauce

3 tablespoons coconut milk, or enough to make a paste

Red Curry Paste

Some folks prefer the tartness of green curry, others the pungency of red.

1. Place all the ingredients in a food processor or blender.

2. Purée into a smooth paste, adding a little more coconut milk if necessary.

3. Taste and adjust seasoning. If it's too salty, add more lime juice. Add extra chili for more spice.

4. Place in an airtight container. In the refrigerator, it will keep for about 1 week.

Sakay

INGREDIENTS | YIELDS ABOUT 1 CUP

¾ cup chili powder

1 tablespoon ground ginger

1 teaspoon cayenne pepper

1 teaspoon ground cumin

4 garlic cloves, peeled and minced

2 teaspoons salt

1 cup peanut or vegetable oil

Sakay is the everyday hot sauce of choice in the African island nation of Madagascar. The flavors represent the country's long history of African, Arab, and Indonesian settlers. Try this on grilled meats and sandwiches.

1. In a sauté pan over medium heat, toast the chili powder, ginger, cayenne, cumin, and garlic until they are nice and fragrant, about 1–2 minutes. Remove from heat and let cool.

2. Put the spice mix in a food processor, add the salt, and blend well. While the blender is still running, slowly pour the oil in a steady stream until a paste is formed.

3. Store in an airtight container in the refrigerator for up to 2 weeks.

1 tablespoon shrimp paste (available at Asian markets)

½ cup red jalapeño or Fresno chilies, seeded and thinly sliced

1 teaspoon sugar

2 tablespoons fresh lime juice

Salt, to taste

Sambal

In Malaysia and Indonesia, sambal is essential to cooking. There are endless sambal variations; it is the cornerstone of many dishes. This basic but very pungent sambal recipe is wonderful on eggs, or grilled chicken and fish.

1. In a saucepan over medium heat, heat the shrimp paste until it dries slightly, about 2 minutes. Make sure to turn the stove fan on, as this will produce a strong scent. Remove from heat and let cool.

2. Put the rest of the ingredients into a food processor. Add the shrimp paste then blend into a smooth paste.

3. Transfer to an airtight container and keep in the refrigerator for up to 1 week.

Shrimp Paste

Shrimp Paste is a common ingredient in Southeast Asian cuisine. While it's a new ingredient to many Westerners, it's used daily in Thailand, Malaysia, Singapore, Indonesia, Vietnam, and the Philippines. The paste is made from ground, fermented shrimp and has a delightfully strong taste and smell—a little goes a long way. Shrimp paste should be easy to find at any Asian market.

¾ pound fresh red chilies such as Fresno, Holland, or cayenne, seeded and roughly chopped

4 cloves of garlic, peeled and roughly chopped

1¼ teaspoon kosher salt

2 tablespoons palm sugar (available at Asian markets), or 2 tablespoons light brown sugar

¼ cup white vinegar

½ cup water

Homemade Sriracha

Everybody knows Sriracha, aka the Rooster Sauce, *which comes in the clear plastic bottle with a bright green cap. Chefs and home cooks alike use Sriracha in a wide range of dishes. True Sriracha fans might want to take the next step and try making it at home with this quick recipe. Feel free to adjust the garlic or sugar to your liking.*

1. Put the chilies, garlic, salt, sugar, vinegar, and water in small saucepan. Bring to a boil, then lower heat and let simmer for 5 minutes. Remove from heat and let cool to room temperature.

2. Purée the mixture in a blender for about 5 minutes, adding water if necessary, until the sauce is smooth.

3. Strain the sauce into a clean bowl. Taste and adjust seasoning.

4. Transfer sauce to a jar and let sit for a few hours so the flavors can come together. Store in the refrigerator, where it will keep for about 1 month.

8 garlic cloves, peeled and roughly chopped

½ cup parsley leaves and stems, roughly chopped

⅓ cup cilantro leaves and stems, roughly chopped

Grated zest of 2 lemons

4 teaspoons hot paprika

2 teaspoons chili powder

2 teaspoons ground cumin

1 cup olive oil

Chermoula

Chermoula is a hot sauce used all over northern Africa. It's especially popular in Morocco and Tunisia, where it is most commonly used as a spice rub for fish. It has a wonderful citrus flavor and is also nice on grilled chicken and pork.

1. Combine all the ingredients except for oil in a blender. Purée on low until it forms a course paste.

2. With the blender running, slowly add oil in a steady stream until a smooth, thick paste forms.

3. Store in an airtight container in the refrigerator for up to 2 weeks.

1 bunch of flat-leaf parsley, roughly chopped

4 garlic cloves, peeled and roughly chopped

2 tablespoons fresh oregano, roughly chopped (you could also use dried oregano, in which case 1 teaspoon will be plenty)

½ cup olive oil

2 tablespoons red wine vinegar

½ teaspoon red pepper flakes

Salt and pepper, to taste

Chimichurri

A staple in Argentina, chimichurri is a quick and easy way to use up a lot of parsley. It gets heat from a little bit of red pepper flakes, but feel free to add more. Chimichurri is magnificent on steaks, but also great on all kinds of meats. It's even delicious tossed with pasta.

1. Place all the ingredients in a blender or food processor and purée until it forms a coarsely ground paste.

2. Serve immediately.

3. Store in an airtight container in the refrigerator for up to 1 month. If the oil solidifies, bring it to room temperature before use.

The Legend of Chimichurri

The exact origin of chimichurri is unknown, but one popular legend is that it is named after an Irishman, Jimmy McCurry, an Argentinian sympathizer who helped fight for the country's independence in the nineteenth century. Supposedly he was the first person to make this sauce, which became wildly popular. Unfortunately, the name *Jimmy McCurry* was hard for natives to pronounce, resulting in the word *chimichurri*.

1 medium eggplant, cut into thick slices

2 red bell peppers, whole

5 cloves of garlic, whole and unpeeled

½ cup olive oil

½ teaspoon salt

1½ teaspoons hot paprika

½ teaspoon red pepper flakes

¼ teaspoon ground cayenne pepper

Black pepper, to taste

1–2 teaspoons fresh lemon juice, or to taste

Avjar

Avjar (pronounced "AYE-var") is a roasted vegetable spread that's a staple of Serbian cuisine. You can serve avjar as a dip for chips, crackers, or flatbread. It also makes a nice addition to sandwiches. Try using smoked paprika for an extra flavor boost.

1. Preheat the oven to 350°F. Place the eggplant, red bell pepper, and garlic on a baking sheet. Roast the vegetables for 1–2 hours until they are brown and soft (the eggplant should be collapsed), turning every 20 minutes.

2. Remove the vegetables from the oven and let cool. When the vegetables are cool, peel them. Discard the skins as well as the pepper seeds and core.

3. Roughly chop the vegetables and add to a blender or food processor.

4. Add the remaining ingredients and process until it forms a thick, smooth paste.

5. Store in an airtight container in the refrigerator for up to 2 weeks.

INGREDIENTS | YIELDS 2 CUPS

½ cup pumpkin seeds

1 tablespoon vegetable oil

½ cup chopped onion

2 cloves garlic, minced

5 jalapeño peppers

1 cup cilantro leaves

1 cup flat leaf parsley

2 tablespoons lime juice

½ teaspoon salt

¼ teaspoon pepper

½ cup olive oil

⅓ cup grated Manchego or Romano cheese

Jalapeño Pesto

This pesto can be tossed with some hot cooked pasta for an instant lunch, or mixed with sour cream for an easy appetizer. It also freezes well, in ice cube trays, and keeps for about 3 months when frozen.

1. In small skillet, toast pumpkin seeds over medium heat until light brown and fragrant. Remove to kitchen towel to cool. In same skillet, heat vegetable oil and sauté onion and garlic until tender. Remove to blender or food processor bowl.

2. Add cooled seeds, jalapeños, cilantro, parsley, lime juice, salt, and pepper and blend or process until finely chopped. With motor running, add olive oil in a thin stream until a paste forms. Remove to bowl and stir in cheese.

3. Cover with plastic wrap and refrigerate up to 2 days, or freeze up to 3 months.

Nut Substitutions

Other nuts can be substituted for pumpkin seeds. Peanuts, pine nuts, and slivered almonds have about the same texture and similar flavor. For a richer flavor, use pecans or cashews. Remember to let all nuts cool thoroughly after roasting and before chopping or processing, or they will be soggy.

½ cup smooth peanut butter

½ cup water

1 tablespoon minced red chili pepper (jalapeño or serrano)

2 garlic cloves, minced

2 teaspoons brown sugar

1 teaspoon grated fresh ginger

2 teaspoons lemon juice

1 tablespoon soy sauce

2 tablespoons chopped peanuts

Indonesian Peanut Sauce

Satay: whether it's chicken, beef, pork, or shrimp, this is the sauce to serve with it for dipping.

1. Heat the peanut butter and water in a sauce pan over low heat, whisking to smooth out the peanut butter.

2. Add the chili pepper, garlic, brown sugar, ginger, and lemon juice and continue to cook over low heat for a few minutes, stirring to prevent scorching.

3. Stir in the soy sauce and remove from heat.

4. Stir in the chopped peanuts.

5. Serve with a variety of things such as skewered shrimp, chicken, beef, or pork.

4 egg yolks

1 tablespoon cold water

8 ounces butter, melted

1 tablespoon lemon juice

2 cans chipotle peppers, puréed

Salt, to taste

White pepper, to taste

Chipotle Hollandaise Sauce

Put this sauce in a thermos to keep it warm while you prepare the food it will be served with. Spicy Eggs Benedict, anyone?

1. Whisk egg yolks and water in a stainless steel or glass bowl over simmering water and cook until mixture thickens. Be careful not to overcook or scramble the yolks.

2. Slowly pour the melted butter into the yolks, drop by drop at first, whisking constantly to form an emulsion. Pour the butter in a thin stream after the emulsion gets started and the sauce starts to thicken; continue whisking.

3. Remove bowl from heat and whisk in the lemon juice and chipotle pepper purée.

4. Season sauce with salt and white pepper to taste.

3 large plum tomatoes

2 large red bell peppers

1 medium onion, halved

1 dried ancho chili

½ cup sliced almonds

3 garlic cloves, peeled and smashed

2 tablespoons sherry vinegar

1 slice toasted white bread (or day old bread) cut into cubes

1 tablespoon Spanish smoked paprika

¼ teaspoon cayenne pepper

¼ cup olive oil plus more for sautéing

Salt and pepper, to taste

Romesco Sauce

Romesco is a classic Spanish sauce that originates in Catalonia. Traditionally it's made with the nyora peppers grown in the region, though here you can substitute roasted red peppers.

1. Heat oven to 400°F. Put tomatoes, bell peppers, and onion in a baking dish and drizzle with olive oil. Roast until charred and soft, turning once or twice, about 40 minutes. Remove from oven, set aside to cool.

2. Over medium-high heat, heat a splash of olive oil in a small skillet. Add ancho chili and dry until it puffs slightly and gets a shade darker, about 1 minute. Transfer to a bowl and cover with boiling water. Let stand until chili is softened, 15–30 minutes.

3. When vegetables are cool enough to handle, peel and seed tomatoes and red peppers, and roughly chop the onion. Seed the ancho chili. Place everything in a blender.

4. Over medium-high heat, heat another splash of olive oil in skillet and add almonds. Cook until lightly toasted, about 1–2 minutes. Add almonds to blender.

5. To the blender, add ¼ cup olive oil, garlic, vinegar, bread, smoked paprika, and cayenne. Purée until it is smooth, but still rough textured.

6. Transfer Romesco sauce to a bowl and season to taste with salt and pepper.

INGREDIENTS | YIELDS 1 CUP

2 tablespoons olive oil

6 garlic cloves, peeled and finely minced

2 Scotch bonnet or Habanero peppers, seeded and finely chopped

1 tablespoon ground allspice

1 teaspoon ground cinnamon

2 tablespoons brown sugar

1 teaspoon white pepper

1 tablespoon dried thyme

1 teaspoon salt

1 teaspoon ground ginger

4 scallions, roughly chopped

⅔ cup fresh lime juice

¼ cup red wine vinegar

Jerk Sauce

Jerk, a fiery sauce that is brushed onto barbecue chicken, pork, beef, and seafood, originates in Jamaica. It's supposed to be very spicy, so don't be shy about using those peppers. This recipe will give you a thick paste good for rubbing onto meats.

1. Heat the oil in a small skillet. Add the garlic and chili peppers and sauté until garlic begins to brown. Add allspice, cinnamon, and brown sugar. Cook, stirring constantly, until the sugar melts and mixture beings to clump. Remove from heat and let cool.

2. Put sugar mixture into a blender. Add remaining ingredients and blend until it forms a smooth paste.

3. Refrigerate in an airtight container where it will keep for 2 weeks.

Vinegars

The word *vinegar* comes from the French *vin aigre*, which means sour wine. Throughout history, it has been one of the most important elements in food preservation. Vinegars come in all sorts of flavors—red wine, champagne, raspberry, balsamic—and can add both acidity and complexity to dishes.

CHAPTER 7

Salsas

1 white onion, finely chopped

4 ripe tomatoes, seeded and finely chopped

3 jalapeño peppers, seeded and finely chopped

½ cup cilantro leaves, finely chopped

1 tablespoon fresh lime juice

Salt, to taste

Pico de Gallo

A classic, fresh salsa that's easy to throw together just minutes before eating. This salsa tastes best in summer, when tomatoes are at their juiciest and most flavorful. For more spice, don't seed the chili peppers.

1. Combine all the ingredients in a bowl and mix thoroughly.

2. If there is time, let it sit in the refrigerator for 20 minutes.

Pico de Gallo: What's in a Name?

Pico de Gallo translates literally to "the beak of the rooster." The exact reason why is unknown, though perhaps it's because the red of the tomatoes is reminiscent of the bird's beak. Pico de Gallo is also beloved because it contains the three colors of the Mexican flag: red, white, and green.

1 pound tomatillos

2 garlic cloves

3 scallions

3 dried chiles de arbol

1 handful cilantro

Dried oregano, to taste

Salt, to taste

Roasted Tomatillo Salsa

This is a relatively simple salsa, but taking the time to roast the tomatillos, chilies, garlic, and scallions gives the salsa an extra smoky and charred flavor that is well worth the extra time.

1. Remove the papery husks from the tomatillos and wash thoroughly.

2. Peel the garlic, but leave the cloves whole. Trim the root ends off the scallions.

3. On a comal or nonstick skillet, roast the tomatillos, chilies, garlic, and scallions until the tomatillos are softened and blackened.

4. Put all the vegetables into a blender with the cilantro, oregano, and salt. Blend until smooth.

5. Store in an airtight container in the refrigerator where it will keep for up to 2 weeks.

What Is a *Comal*?

A *comal* is a smooth, flat griddle, usually cast iron, used throughout Mexico and Latin America to cook tortillas, toast spices, and roast chilies and vegetables. In many cultures, the comal is handed down from generation to generation, with the idea that the comal becomes better and more seasoned with age. If you don't have a comal, no worries, a cast iron pan will do.

Mango Habanero Salsa

This is a great salsa to enjoy in the summer. The juicy sweet mangoes offer a nice contrast to the ultra-hot habanero pepper.

INGREDIENTS | YIELDS ABOUT 4 CUPS

3 tablespoons canola oil

3 whole cloves garlic, unpeeled

3 tomatillos, husked and washed

3 tomatoes, cored

1 red bell pepper

1 yellow bell pepper

1 orange habanero chili

1 medium red onion, finely chopped

¼ cup chopped cilantro leaves

¼ cup fresh lime juice

1 large mango, peeled, pitted, and cut into ¼" cubes

Kosher salt, to taste

1. Set oven to broil. Place a rack 6" from the heat source. Put the oil, garlic, tomatillos, tomatoes, bell peppers, chili, and onion in a large bowl and toss.

2. Transfer the ingredients to a foil-lined baking sheet. Broil them, turning a few times, until they are charred and blistered, about 10 minutes.

3. Transfer all but the peppers and chilies to a bowl; let cool. Continue broiling the peppers and chilies until soft, 3–5 minutes longer. Remove chilies from oven and let them steam in a covered bowl for a few minutes.

4. Peel the garlic. Stem, seed, and peel peppers and chilies. Transfer all the roasted vegetables to a blender or food processor. Process until finely chopped.

5. Transfer the salsa to a bowl and stir in red onions, cilantro, lime juice, and mangoes. Season with salt.

½ pound Roma tomatoes

½ pound tomatillos, husked and washed

1 cup (between 30–40) chiles de arbol

½ bunch cilantro, leaves only, roughly chopped

1 medium white onion, chopped

4 garlic cloves, peeled and lightly smashed

2 cups water

1 teaspoon salt

Chile de Arbol Salsa

Chiles de arbol are a staple in many salsas because of their strong heat and naturally subtle, smoky flavor. This salsa puts those flavors at the forefront.

1. Set oven to broil. Place tomatoes and tomatillos on a baking sheet. Broil, turning occasionally, until they are charred, 10–12 minutes. Transfer to a saucepan.

2. Add the remaining ingredients to a large saucepan. Bring mixture to a boil and cook until the onion is soft, about 12 minutes.

3. Transfer the sauce to a blender or food processor. Purée until smooth.

4. Strain the salsa into a bowl.

5. Store leftover salsa in the refrigerator, where it will keep for about a week.

2 cups diced fresh pineapple

½ cup chopped cilantro

¼ cup red onion, finely chopped

1 serrano pepper, seeded and finely chopped

Juice and zest of 1 lime

¼ teaspoon kosher salt

Pineapple Salsa

Another great tropical salsa that's especially nice in the summer. If you can, let it sit for 30 minutes before serving to give all the flavors time to mix.

1. Toss all the ingredients together in a large bowl and mix well.

2. Serve immediately or cover and chill until ready to use.

1 pound (around 20) tomatillos, husked and washed

4 serrano chilies, seeded and roughly chopped

1 cup cilantro leaves and stems, roughly chopped

1 large garlic clove, peeled and roughly chopped

Raw Tomatillo Salsa

This simple salsa, called cruda, *is probably the easiest way to make a salsa from tomatillos. This sauce may seem a bit thin at first, but it will thicken as it stands.*

1. Put the tomatillos in a small pan, just barely cover them with water, and bring to a simmer. Simmer for about 10 minutes or until they are softened. Drain, but reserve a bit of the cooking water.

2. Combine ½ cup of the cooking water, chilies, cilantro, and garlic in a blender. Blend until almost smooth.

3. Add the cooked tomatillos in small batches, blending briefly after each one. The sauce should be chunky and rough.

4. Transfer to a bowl and add salt.

Tomatillos

Tomatillos, called *tomates verdes* or *green tomatoes* in Spanish, are not the same thing as green, unripe tomatoes. While they are in the same family, they are a different genus. Tomatillos grow surrounded by an inedible, paper-like "husk" that must be discarded before cooking.

8 medium red tomatoes

1 yellow onion, halved

4 dried chipotle chilies

2 cloves garlic, peeled

½–1 cup water

Salt, to taste

Smoky Chipotle Salsa

Chipotles add a surprise smoky flavor to this salsa, which also has plenty of sweetness from roasted tomatoes. Serve this as a table salsa with chips for a nice change of pace.

1. Roast tomatoes, onion, chilies, and garlic on a comal or cast iron skillet until they are nearly blackened.

2. Place the vegetables and chilies in a blender and add a little water. Blend until smooth. Season with salt to taste.

1 cup roasted unsalted peanuts, shelled

2 cups water, separated

4 canned chipotle chilies in adobo, roughly chopped

2 garlic cloves, peeled and roughly chopped

2 black peppercorns

2 cloves

2 tablespoons pork lard or vegetable oil

Salt, to taste

Peanut Salsa

This unusual salsa originates on the gulf coast of Mexico. Spread this sauce on top of warm tortillas or rice.

1. Grind the peanuts in a coffee grinder or food processor until they are a fine powder.

2. Put ½ cup of water into the blender, along with the chilies, garlic, and spices. Blend well.

3. Heat the lard or vegetable oil, then fry the blended ingredients in it for 4 minutes, stirring constantly so they do not stick to the bottom. Gradually stir in the ground peanuts and cook for another 2 minutes.

4. Add the rest of the water and salt and continue cooking, stirring and scraping the bottom of the pan, for another 5 minutes.

1 cup pumpkin seeds (pepitas), toasted

3 tomatoes

½ large white onion, thickly sliced

1 habanero chili

½ cup cilantro leaves

Salt, to taste

Water as needed

Creamy Pumpkin Seed and Habanero Salsa

This salsa, called sikil pak, *is a traditional Mayan recipe from the Yucatan Peninsula. It's incredibly creamy, yet there is no trace of dairy. Be careful when handling the roasted habanero here— consider gloves!*

1. Toast the pepitas in a dry, hot skillet or in the oven until golden brown.

2. Char the tomatoes, onion, and habanero on a comal or cast-iron skillet until they are softened and a little black, about 5 minutes. Carefully seed and roughly chop the habanero.

3. Put all the ingredients into a food processor or blender. Pulse until well blended. The salsa should be thick and creamy. Add a little water to thin if necessary.

4 large shrimp, unshelled, preferably with heads still on

2 medium tomatoes

2 jalapeño chilies

Salt, to taste

2 tablespoons olive oil

Shrimp Salsa

This delightful, unexpected salsa will be a hit with seafood lovers. It's delicious with tortilla chips. Add a little extra olive oil and serve it as a spread with warm tortillas.

1. Set the oven to broil. Place shrimp, tomatoes, and jalapeños on a baking sheet and broil. Remove shrimp when they are cooked, about 2–3 minutes. Continue broiling the tomatoes and jalapeños until they are softened and charred, another 4–5 minutes. Remove and set aside to cool.

2. Peel, remove the heads, and devein the shrimp. Chop roughly.

3. Gently mash all the ingredients together, including the salt and olive oil, either by hand or on a low blender setting.

4. Transfer to a bowl and serve at room temperature.

INGREDIENTS | YIELDS 1½ CUP

1 poblano chili, seeded and finely chopped

1 red jalapeño, seeded and finely chopped

2 yellow chilies (such as a guero or Anaheim), seeded and finely chopped

2 serrano chilies, seeds intact, finely chopped

½ white onion, finely chopped

2 tomatoes, seeded and finely chopped

3 tablespoons fresh lime juice

½ teaspoon dried oregano

Salt, to taste

Mixed Chili Salsa

This raw salsa is bright and colorful. If you are lucky enough to live near a market that sells a variety of chilies, be sure to make this. Feel free to vary it with whatever chilies are fresh and available.

1. Mix all the ingredients together in a non-reactive bowl.

2. Set aside for 1 hour before serving.

Guero

Guero chilies are medium-hot peppers that are a yellow color. They are also sometimes called *gold-spike chilies*. *Guero* translates from Spanish to *blonde*, though it is also called out on the streets in Mexico as a generic nickname (not necessarily derogative) for light-haired or light-skinned people and tourists.

3 tablespoons vegetable oil

2 garlic cloves, finely chopped

2 cups jalapeños, seeded, and cut into very fine strips

2 cups white onion, finely sliced

1 cup chicken broth (you can also use water, though broth adds more flavor)

Salt, to taste

8 ounces queso fresco or mild Cheddar

Salsa Ranchera

Here's a salsa for cheese lovers. This warm, creamy salsa is great with grilled meats, or serve it as an appetizer with warm tortillas or chips.

1. Heat oil in a skillet. Add the garlic and sauté, then add the chilies and onions. Cook them at low-medium heat until the onions are just beginning to brown.

2. Add the broth and cook over medium heat until the onions and chilies are softened and thoroughly cooked. Add salt to taste.

3. Place the cheese on top and cover the pan.

4. Serve as soon as the cheese is melted.

Queso Fresco

Queso fresco translates to *fresh cheese*. It has a crumbly texture and sharp flavor that is reminiscent of a mild feta. Be sure to get whole milk queso fresco because it will melt better. Queso fresco is also great crumbled over tacos.

Roasted Corn Salsa

This is a great salsa to make in summer, when corn on the cob is bursting with sweetness. You can serve with chips or put it on tacos, but it's also hearty enough to be a side dish.

INGREDIENTS | YIELDS 3½ CUPS

3 ears of fresh corn

4 scallions, white and green parts separated and thinly sliced

2 tablespoons unsalted butter

2 cloves garlic, peeled and minced

2 plum tomatoes, seeded and finely diced

2 fresh jalapeños, with seeds, finely diced

1½ teaspoons kosher salt, separated

1½ teaspoons ground cumin, separated

1 teaspoon chili powder, separated

Salt and pepper, to taste

1. Shuck the corn cobs and shave the corn kernels from the cob. Heat a dry large cast-iron skillet over medium-high heat and pan-roast corn, stirring occasionally, until golden brown, about 8–9 minutes. Transfer to a bowl.

2. Cook the white part of scallions in butter with garlic, 1 teaspoon of salt, ½ teaspoon each of cumin and chili powder, and a few pinches of black pepper. Cook until scallions are tender, about 3 minutes.

3. Remove pan from heat and stir in corn, tomatoes, jalapeños, and spices.

4. Transfer to bowl. Serve warm or chill in the refrigerator first.

½ pound dried guajillo chilies

3 cups water

5 large cloves of garlic, roasted

1 teaspoon ground cumin

1 teaspoon kosher salt

½ pound Roma tomatoes

2 teaspoons toasted pumpkin seeds

⅓ cup apple cider vinegar

1 teaspoon dried oregano

Guajillo Salsa

This is a salsa of medium heat, with plenty of nice chili flavor from the guajillos. You can serve it as a table salsa or heat it with two tablespoons of oil or lard to make a hot sauce to serve with meat.

1. Remove the stems from the guajillos and lightly toast them on a comal or cast iron skillet. Transfer them to a bowl and cover with hot water. Let them sit for at least 15 minutes.

2. When the chilies are softened, remove them from the water and chop roughly. Save a bit of the chili soaking water.

3. Purée the chilies with the remaining ingredients until the mixture forms a paste. Add a little chili water to thin if necessary.

Pumpkin Seeds

Called *pepitas* in Spanish, pumpkin seeds are commonly used in Mexican cuisine as a thickener for sauces. Along with adding body to salsas and moles, pumpkin seeds add a warm, nutty flavor to dishes.

6 tomatillos, husked and washed, coarsely chopped

2 jalapeños, coarsely chopped

3 garlic cloves

3 medium-sized ripe avocados, peeled, pitted, and thinly sliced

5 sprigs cilantro

1 teaspoon salt

1½ cups Mexican crema (or crème fraiche or sour cream)

Avocado Salsa

This is a tangy green salsa made smooth and silky by the addition of avocados. You can use it on tacos or in enchiladas, but you just might find yourself eating it straight with a spoon. Be sure to use soft, ripe avocados.

1. Combine the tomatillos, jalapeños, and garlic in a saucepan, along with a bit of water. Bring to a boil, then reduce heat and simmer for 10 minutes. Remove from heat and let cool a bit.

2. Place the mixture, along with avocados, cilantro, and salt in a food processor or blender. Blend until smooth. Add a little water if necessary to loosen mixture from blender blades.

3. Pour into a bowl and stir in the sour cream or crema.

Mexican Crema

Mexican crema, a cultured cream that many people make at home, is similar to sour cream, but not the same. Crema is less thick and less sour, with just a bit of sweetness. It is also more heat-stable than sour cream, though you could easily interchange the two in cooking.

2 jalapeño peppers, minced

1 habanero pepper, minced

1 green bell pepper, minced

4 cloves garlic, minced

1 red onion, chopped

5 ripe tomatoes, chopped

3 tablespoons lemon juice

¼ teaspoon salt

⅛ teaspoon white pepper

¼ cup chopped fresh cilantro

Super Spicy Salsa

You can use salsa in so many ways. It's wonderful in frittatas and delicious as a garnish for chili or grilled chicken.

1. In large bowl, combine jalapeños, habanero pepper, bell pepper, garlic, red onion, and tomatoes.

2. In small bowl, combine lemon juice, salt, and pepper; stir to dissolve salt. Add to tomato mixture along with cilantro.

3. Cover and refrigerate for 3–4 hours before serving.

1 cup red onion

¼ cup cilantro

¼ cup parsley

1 jalapeño pepper

1½ cups black beans, cooked

4 cups tomatoes, chopped

3 tablespoons lime juice

2 tablespoons olive oil

Freshly ground black pepper

Zesty Black Bean Salsa

This is a hearty, filling salsa that gets its body from fiber-rich black beans.

1. Place onion, cilantro, parsley, and jalapeño in food processor; finely chop.

2. In medium bowl, combine onion mixture, black beans, and tomatoes.

3. In separate small bowl, whisk together lime juice, olive oil, and fresh ground pepper. Pour over beans; mix well. Chill before serving.

Using Canned Beans Versus Cooking Your Own

Canned beans are very convenient and can save you time. Keep in mind sodium content of recipes will be higher with canned beans. Reduce sodium content in canned beans by draining and thoroughly rinsing with cold water before using.

CHAPTER 8

Canned Heat: An Overview of Bottled Sauces

People's craving for hot sauce is growing. Over the last few years, sales of hot sauce in the United States have risen by 10 percent each year. The growing market for hot sauces is filled with major players and boutique hot sauce producers from every region of the country and every part of the world. A seemingly infinite number of small manufacturers produce often extremely hot sauces, with names that reflect the intensity inside. Yet while many smaller hot sauce brands have garnered fans and built loyal followings, there are some hot sauces so ubiquitous they have become household names.

A Peek at the Hot Sauce Industry

It's very difficult to get exact facts and figures about the bottled hot sauce industry. Many big corporations that produce hot sauces include them under a broader category of "food," so it's hard to separate out just exactly how much of their sales come from their fiery liquid foodstuffs. Still, some estimate hot sauce sales at around $200 million per year in the United States alone. That's a lot of $3–$6 bottles.

The five large producers in the hot sauce industry are all household names in some part of the country, and some have global notoriety. Tabasco and Louisiana Hot Sauce are privately owned, family companies that are based, you guessed it, in Louisiana. Texas Pete, a red pepper sauce hailing from North Carolina, is another family-owned company. Rounding out the top five are Cholula, a Mexican original created near Guadalajara, and Frank's Red Hot, which also started in Louisiana. Large multinational corporations now own both Cholula and Frank's Red Hot. These five brands control the majority of the hot sauce market.

Many other hot sauces are important industry players, often dominant ones within particular regions or niches. Crystal, Tapatio, Sriracha, Valentina, Trappey's—the list goes on—are North American mainstays, but every country and every part of the world has its own frontrunners and regional favorites. The hot sauce market is expanding and globalizing, and as interest in new cuisines from Asia and Latin America grows throughout the United States, both the demographic profile of hot sauce lovers and the types of hot sauce that people seek are changing by the year.

QUESTION

Who's making all this hot sauce?
It seems like everyone is getting in on the hot sauce making game, including inmates at the Hillsborough County Jail in Florida. At this minimum security prison near Tampa, inmates grow pepper plants as part of a vocational program designed to give them real world job skills. With names like Jailhouse Fire and No Escape, these prisoners haven't given up their sense of humor and are proud to produce and sell a product they claim is "created with conviction."

The Tabasco Story

While new players are changing the hot sauce game every day, some things remain the same. Possibly the most famous hot sauce around the world, Tabasco, has been produced since 1868 in its original location on Avery Island, Louisiana. What's more, it's still made by the same family-owned business, the McIlhenny Company, founded by Edmund McIlhenny.

According to family history, Edmund McIlhenny was a one-time banker and avid gardener who received Tabasco peppers from Central America or Mexico as a gift. Sometime in the mid–to-late 1860s he began producing red peppers from those seeds, and he began to believe that the flavor and spice he found in those peppers would be a great addition to the regional cuisine.

While peppers were foreign to Avery Island, salt was not. In fact, Avery Island rises above the swamps and bayous of the Gulf Coast because it sits on a massive mound of rock salt, which was first discovered by American Indians who traded the salt throughout the region. McIlhenny mashed his crushed red peppers with refined Avery Island salt and aged the mixture for thirty days. He then added white wine vinegar, let the mixture age for another month, strained it and packaged it in small corked bottles.

QUESTION

How do you know if a Tabasco pepper is ripe for the picking?
Tabasco pepper pickers on Avery Island are instructed to pick at the peak of ripeness, when they are most juicy. To ensure that workers are picking the best peppers available, they are given *le petit bâton rouge*, a small wooden dowel that has been painted a bright shade of red that is the preferred pepper hue of the Tabasco brand.

The hot sauce was well received, and McIlhenny decided to expand his pepper crop and market the vinegary-pepper sauce to grocers in New Orleans and around the Gulf Coast region. It is said that McIlhenny first sold bottled Tabasco sauce for $1 per bottle wholesale in 1868, a fairly steep price in inflationary terms, especially when compared to a 2011 retail price of around $3 per 2-ounce bottle.

Now, over 140 years later, Tabasco Sauce is sold in more than 160 countries and territories. Little has changed in its production except for the duration of the aging process, which has lengthened from one month to three years. Some peppers come from places outside of Louisiana, but the sauce is still made on Avery Island. The McIlhenny company's current president is the sixth McIlhenny to have taken the helm, and many of its 200 employees are multi-generational as well.

The Saga of Sriracha

While Tabasco is the old-school mainstay of the hot sauce industry, in the last few years, another American sauce has blazed onto the scene. With its iconic bright green cap and clear plastic bottle emblazoned with a proud, crowing rooster, Sriracha (aka "Rooster Sauce") has emerged as not only a cult favorite, but also a staple sauce with a growing following. Like Tabasco, the story of Sriracha is the story of an American family, albeit an entirely different and modern one.

Sriracha is produced by the Huy Fong Foods company in a suburban factory just east of Los Angeles in California's San Gabriel Valley. The San Gabriel Valley is home to a large number of Asian American immigrants including Huy Fong founder David Tran. Tran, who is Chinese by blood, was raised in Vietnam, where he first began making and selling pepper sate sauce. In 1979, Tran emigrated to the United States on a ship named the Huy Fong. He arrived in Los Angeles in January 1980 and within a month, Huy Fong Foods was born, churning out bottles of his pepper sate sauce.

Business was good. Tran had steady sales, mostly within the Asian immigrant community. He created a few more sauces: a chili garlic sauce; sambal oelek, a paste made from ground fresh chilies; and sambal badjak, a chili paste flavored with onions. His business took a fortuitous turn in 1984, when he created the sauce that would later become a phenomenon.

In 1984, Tran crafted a new hot sauce, a combination of fresh red jalapeños, garlic, sugar, salt, and vinegar, and called it *Sriracha*. Pronounced ("sree-RA-sha") the sauce is named after a village in Thailand that is known for its homemade chili pastes. Tran is the first to admit, though, as he did in a 2009 *New York Times* article about his famed sauce, that "I know it's not Thai Sriracha. It's my Sriracha."

Whatever its origins and influences, Sriracha has taken on a life of its own. Since 1986, Huy Fong has been producing its sauces in a factory in the town of Rosemead, California. Every year since then, it has increased its annual production. Huy Fong has expanded over the years, adding processing and storage facilities, but even that is not enough. Despite the fact that more than ten million bottles of Sriracha are made by Huy Fong each year, they still are not quite able to keep up with demand.

It seems like there is no one out there who isn't using Sriracha. Chain restaurants like P.F. Chang's and Applebee's both feature dishes using the sauce as a major component. Jean-Georges Vongerichten, a renowned chef with restaurants in New York, Paris, Las Vegas, and London, also professes to be a fan who keeps bottles of the sauce in his restaurant kitchens. In 2011, a cookbook dedicated solely to Sriracha-based recipes was published and the cooking magazine *Bon Appetit* ran a feature, "25 Ways to Use Sriracha."

Sriracha has gained such status that the market is now flooded with rooster sauce imitators, all of whom follow the same formula of using an iconic animal to brand the sauce: Cock, Phoenix, and Unicorn brands, to name a few.

Louisiana-Style Hot Sauces

Besides the famed Tabasco family of sauces, there's a veritable army of Louisiana-style hot sauces on the market. What exactly makes a sauce "Louisiana-style"? Typically, these sauces are made with ripe, red tabasco or cayenne peppers. Because of its lush, humid, and hot weather conditions, the state of Louisiana is the ideal environment for chili peppers to thrive. Louisiana sauces are bright red and tangy, usually only adding two other ingredients: vinegar and salt. Occasionally thickeners like xanthan gum are used, but the simple and straightforward Louisiana formula is the general rule.

At Los Angeles Farmers' Market store Light My Fire, hot sauce is the (one-and-only) name of the game. The store stocks over 500 different varieties and also does plenty of business online. Whether it's Louisiana hot sauce, Belizean hot sauce, or novelty hot sauces with names like Dead Man Sauce, Sphincter Shrinker, or simply The Hottest F***ing Sauce, you're likely to find whatever you are looking for. In business for over 15 years, the store also rates hot sauces on a scale of one to ten so you know what you are getting into.

Among the many Louisiana-style sauces out there, the best known include:

- **Crystal Hot Sauce.** Crystal, which claims to be the "#1 Hot Sauce in Louisiana," is easily recognized by its white label crossed with a diagonal blue sash. Crystal is made from fresh cayenne peppers and has been made by Baumer Foods, Inc., since 1923.
- **Frank's Red Hot.** Frank's Red Hot sauce, though it's Louisiana-style, is actually produced in Springfield, Missouri. Originally started in Louisiana in 1920, the company was sold to Durkee Famous Foods, Inc., in 1977, then again to Reckitt Benckiser in 1995. Frank's Red Hot now comes in eight flavors, but the original is the most famous, often cited as the hot sauce used in the creation of the famous Buffalo Wings.
- **Louisiana Hot Sauce.** If you travel in Louisiana, you're likely to find Louisiana brand hot sauce more than any other. Simply packaged, Louisiana's sports a bright yellow label with an iconic red dot and the words "the perfect hot sauce." Louisiana brand is also known for its straight-shooting slogan, "not too hot, not too mild." Louisiana sauce is made from long cayenne peppers that are aged for at least 1 year and is manufactured by Bruce Foods out of New Iberia, Louisiana, which has been making Cajun and Tex-Mex food products since 1928.
- **Trappey's Hot Sauce.** Trappey's Hot Sauce has its own unique tie to the Tabasco empire. In 1898, a former McIlhenny employee named B. F. Trappey began growing tabasco chilies from Avery Island seed. He founded his own company, B. F. Trappey and Sons and began producing his own sauce. Trappey's is now made from red jalapeño peppers

and is manufactured by B&G Foods, Inc., which also produces Cream of Wheat and products from celebrity chef Emeril Lagasse.

- **Texas Pete.** Despite its name, Texas Pete produces one of the bestselling Louisiana-style sauces on the market. Never mind that the family behind Texas Pete is actually from North Carolina. The Garner family started out making barbecue sauce, but soon customers were requesting a spicier sauce. Rather than mess with the original, they created a spicier, Louisiana-style sauce with vinegar and salt, which is now their calling card.

Mexican Hot Sauces

While jarred and canned salsa now outsells every other condiment in the United States, that doesn't mean there isn't room for smoother, bottled Mexican-style hot sauces. Instead of the chunky, tomato-based sauces that you pick up with a tortilla chip, Mexican-style bottled sauces are silky and demand to be shaken out onto eggs and sandwiches, and into soups and stews.

FACT

Salsa, once just a fixture in kitchens and dining tables in Mexico, has become an American staple. It would be more accurate to say that salsa has become America's favorite condiment, since for nearly a decade salsa has outsold ketchup and mayonnaise. Salsa sales are a clear indicator of the trend toward heat and spice in the American palate.

- **Tapatío.** In 2011, the man in the yellow mariachi suit and giant sombrero celebrated his fortieth anniversary. Started in 1971 by Mr. Jose-Luis Saavedra, Sr., Tapatío hot sauce has become a beloved hot sauce in the United States, and mariachi man with the strangely compelling facial expression has become just as popular. To wit, the hot sauce is now carried and distributed by corporate food giant Kraft Foods. The word *tapatio* actually means a person who hails from the city of Guadalajara, Mexico.

- **Valentina.** There's a growing movement among hot sauce enthusiasts who say that while Tapatio is good, Valentina is even better. Valentina sauce isn't just about the heat; there is also a nice, full flavor that comes through the sauce. Valentina, which is produced in a factory in Guadalajara, provides employment for about 125 local families in the area and is becoming more widely available outside of Mexico and throughout the United States.
- **Cholula.** The man on the Tapatio bottle may have a bunch of fans, but so too does the woman on the Cholula hot sauce label. The name Cholula is derived from the pre-Hispanic word *Chollollan* meaning "the place of the retreat." *Cholula* is also the name of a 2,500 year old city in Mexico famous for its many churches. Cholula has been working its way into people's stomachs and hearts because of its restaurant partnership with chains like California Pizza Kitchen, IHOP, Boston Market Chicken, Qdoba Mexican Grill, and On the Border.

CHAPTER 9

Cooking with Bottled Sauce

2 pounds tomatoes

2 red bell peppers

1 big chunk of day-old French bread, crust removed

2 cucumbers, peeled, seeded, and chopped

4 garlic cloves, peeled and finely minced

2 tablespoons sherry vinegar

1–2 tablespoons Tabasco, to taste

½ cup olive oil

1 teaspoon fresh tarragon, minced (or a pinch of dried tarragon)

Salt and back pepper, to taste

Tabasco Gazpacho

By roasting the tomatoes and red peppers first, this cold soup gets an even richer, more concentrated flavor. Using the best quality olive oil you have on hand makes it even better.

1. Heat the oven to 350°F. Put the tomatoes and bell peppers in a baking pan and roast for 30–40 minutes, until they are softened and the peppers are lightly charred. Remove from oven.

2. Transfer roasted vegetables to a large bowl and let sit, covered, for 20–30 minutes to cool.

3. Cut or tear bread into 1" pieces. Soak the bread in a small bowl of water for 10–15 minutes.

4. When vegetables are cool enough to handle, remove peels, stems, and seeds. Do this over a bowl to make sure to catch their juices. Tear the tomatoes and peppers apart into small pieces and return to large bowl. Strain the juices and add to the tomato and pepper mixture.

5. Add cucumbers, garlic, vinegar, Tabasco, and olive oil to bowl.

6. Remove bread from soaking liquid. Do not squeeze out excess liquid. Add bread to bowl, along with tarragon, salt and pepper.

7. Transfer all ingredients to blender and blend until smooth. The soup should be smooth but with a slightly rough texture.

8. Place soup in a serving bowl and refrigerate for at least 3 hours before serving.

12 eggs

¼ cup mayonnaise

2 teaspoons Dijon or spicy brown mustard

1 tablespoon fresh lemon juice

1–2 teaspoons Tabasco, to taste

1 tablespoon onion or shallot, finely minced

Salt and pepper, to taste

Paprika, for garnish

Tabasco Deviled Eggs

An all-American classic, with a little extra kick. These will be a hit at any picnic or barbecue.

1. Hard boil the eggs by putting them in a single layer in the bottom of a saucepan and covering with cold water. Bring to a boil over medium-high heat. When water begins boiling, immediately remove pan from heat and let stand, covered, for 12 minutes. Drain eggs and rinse under cold water. Set aside to cool for 15 minutes.

2. Peel eggs and cut in half lengthwise. Scoop yolks out into bowl. Mash yolks with fork and mix them with all ingredients except paprika.

3. Fill whites with spoonful of yolk mixture. Cover and chill.

4. To serve, sprinkle paprika on top of yolk mixture.

1½ pounds ground beef

1 teaspoon kosher salt

¼ teaspoon ground black pepper

2–4 tablespoons Sriracha, depending on your taste

¼ cup onion, finely minced

Sriracha Burgers

For even more Sriracha flavor, slather these burgers with Sriracha Aioli (recipe follows).

1. Combine all ingredients in a large bowl. Stir gently until just combined.

2. Shape meat into 4 burgers, about 4"–5" wide.

3. Start your grill. If you are cooking on a stovetop, heat a cast iron skillet over medium-high heat for 3–4 minutes until it is very, very hot.

4. Put burgers on grill or in pan and cook for 4–5 minutes per side, depending on your preference for doneness. Four minutes per side should yield medium-rare burgers.

5. Remove burgers from heat and serve immediately on buns with your choice of toppings.

Building a Better Burger

Once you start making burgers by hand, you're probably not going to want to stop. Season your meat to suit our own tastes. Good additions to burgers include: minced fresh herbs such as parsley or basil, peeled and minced fresh ginger, soy sauce, and cumin. Just stir the ingredients in gently. For best results, you want to handle the meat as little as possible so as not to smush and compress it.

1 large egg yolk

½–1 tablespoon Sriracha, depending on your taste

1 garlic clove, peeled and finely minced

Pinch of salt

½ cup olive oil

Lemon juice, to taste (optional)

Sriracha Aioli

Aioli *is basically just a fancy way of saying mayonnaise with garlic in it. Use this Sriracha-tinged sauce as you would mayonnaise, but also as a dipping sauce for French fries.*

1. Combine all ingredients except oil and lemon juice in a blender.

2. Turn blender on and pour oil through the top in a thin stream until the mixture has the consistency of mayonnaise. Taste; add lemon juice and adjust seasoning to taste.

INGREDIENTS | YIELDS ½ CUP

½ cup kosher salt

6–8 teaspoons Sriracha, depending on your taste

Sriracha Salt

Sprinkle this spicy (and not to mention pretty) salt on anything you want to have a little more flavor and heat. Or try it on the rim of a Bloody Mary.

1. In a bowl, mix together salt and Sriracha. Stir well.

2. Line a baking sheet with parchment paper and spread the salt out in as thin a layer as possible. Let sit on the counter, stirring a couple of times, until salt is completely dry. (This should take about 1–2 days.)

3. Transfer salt to an airtight container, breaking up any clumps that may have formed.

Keeping It Kosher

What's the difference between kosher salt and table salt? Yes, both are salts and give pretty much the same flavor, but kosher salt, unlike table salt, has no additives. Table salt is iodized and so has additives like potassium or sodium iodide. You may not notice a taste difference, but some say the additives give table salt a slightly metallic flavor. Kosher salt is also made up of larger, more coarse grains of salt, which makes it easier to pick up in a pinch, making it a favorite of chefs.

Sauce

2 tablespoons white vinegar

¼ cup curry powder

¼ cup soy sauce

1 cup oyster sauce

¼ cup Sriracha sauce

¼ cup ketchup

Remaining Ingredients

2 gallons water

1 pound rice stick noodles

4 tablespoons canola oil

½ pound medium-size shrimp

8 ounces julienned chicken

1 tablespoon chopped garlic

1 cup julienned cabbage

½ cup julienned carrots

2 medium diced tomatoes

1 bunch sliced green onions

⅓ cup shallots

¼ bunch roughly chopped cilantro

1 teaspoon sesame oil

1 quartered lime

Sriracha Noodles

Sriracha adds a wonderful kick to this noodle dish. You could also eliminate the chicken or shrimp and add in your favorite protein for a change.

1. In a bowl, combine all the ingredients for the sauce, mix well, and set aside.

2. Bring water to a rolling boil. Place rice sticks in boiling water for 2 minutes. Drain, then rinse under rapid running hot water for 1 minute, and drain well again. Toss noodles with 2 tablespoons of canola oil and set aside.

3. In a hot wok, stir-fry shrimp and chicken in 2 tablespoons canola oil until just done, about 2 minutes.

4. Add garlic, cabbage, carrots, and tomatoes and stir-fry for 1 minute.

5. Add noodles and stir-fry 1 minute more.

6. Add 1 cup vinegar mixture and stir-fry until ingredients are well incorporated, about 2 minutes. Add onions, shallots, cilantro, lime juice and sesame oil and toss briefly.

24 chicken wings

Vegetable oil, for frying

½ cup butter

1 cup Louisiana-style hot sauce

5 celery ribs, cut into 3" segments

Blue cheese dressing

Buffalo Chicken Wings

Use any bottled Louisiana-style hot sauce you like, such as Frank's Red Hot or Louisiana Brand. But FYI, Frank's is known as the original buffalo wing sauce.

1. Wash the chicken wings, drain, and pat dry. Cut the tips off the wings and discard.

2. Heat a skillet with about 2" of oil. Heat to 400°F.

3. Fry chicken wings until they are cooked inside and golden brown and crispy on the outside. Transfer to a plate lined with a paper towel to absorb excess oil.

4. Melt butter and hot sauce together in a small saucepan over low-medium heat.

5. Toss chicken wings and sauce together in a large bowl. Serve with celery and blue cheese dressing.

Buffalo Wings

No one is exactly sure about how Buffalo wings were born, but one thing everyone does agree on is that they were created in Buffalo, New York. Most legends are based out of the Anchor Bar, where owner Teressa Bellissimo is credited for frying up the chicken wings and tossing them in a spicy sauce to serve to late-night patrons. Everyone also agrees that Buffalo wings taste best when served with celery sticks and blue cheese dressing, to cut the heat.

1¼ cups mayonnaise

¼ cup stone-ground or Dijon mustard

1 teaspoon Frank's Red Hot sauce

1 garlic clove, peeled and roughly chopped

1 tablespoon pickle juice

1 tablespoon capers (optional)

1 teaspoon horseradish

½ teaspoon hot paprika

Spicy Remoulade Sauce

Remoulade is a fixture in New Orleans, where it is slathered on po' boy sandwiches. Try this smeared on any sandwich you like.

Combine all ingredients in a food processor. Process until mostly smooth.

Remoulade

The classic Remoulade is a French sauce made by combining mayonnaise (typically homemade), mustard, herbs, anchovies, and capers or cornichon pickles. Traditionally, it's served chilled as an accompaniment to cold meat or fish. Remoulade took on a life of its own in Louisiana, where it became pink and infused with local chilies.

1 cup soy sauce

1 cup brown sugar

2 cloves garlic, peeled and finely minced

2 tablespoons smooth peanut butter

Juice of 2 fresh lemons

1 tablespoon Sambal Oelek hot sauce

4 pounds boneless, country-style pork ribs, cut into ½"-thick cubes

Spicy Filipino Barbecue Skewers

While not as well-known as other types of barbecue, Filipino barbecue is a total crowd favorite. It gets a little extra sweetness from peanut butter and should caramelize and crisp nicely on a grill.

1. Combine soy sauce, brown sugar, and garlic in medium saucepan. Bring to a boil, then reduce heat to a simmer, stirring until sugar is dissolved.

2. Remove sauce from heat. Add peanut butter, lemon, and hot sauce. Stir to combine and let cool.

3. Place pork in a large bowl or zip-top bag and pour marinade over it. Cover or seal and let meat marinate in the refrigerator for at least 3 hours, overnight if possible.

4. Remove meat from refrigerator 1 hour before cooking and let come to room temperature. If using bamboo skewers for grilling, soak them in cold water to prevent burning.

5. Turn your grill on. Grill directly over a hot fire, turning meat every 3–5 minutes until each side is nicely browned and meat is cooked through.

¼ cup fresh lime juice

¼ teaspoon kosher salt

½–1 teaspoon Tapatio hot sauce, depending on your taste

1 clove garlic, peeled and finely minced

¼ teaspoon ground cumin

¾ cup olive oil

1 cup quinoa, cooked

1 (15-ounce) can of black beans, drained

½ red onion, finely chopped

2 cups cherry tomatoes, cut into quarters

1 large carrot, peeled and finely chopped

⅓ cup fresh cilantro leaves, finely chopped

Black Bean Salad with Tapatio Vinaigrette

Tapatio, cilantro, black beans, and cumin give this salad a fresh but decidedly south-of-the-border flavor.

1. Make the vinaigrette. Combine lime juice, salt, Tapatio, garlic, cumin, and olive oil in small bowl or jar. Stir or shake to combine. Taste and adjust seasonings to your liking.

2. Cook the quinoa. Wash it very thoroughly (if you do not wash quinoa before cooking it will have an unpleasant, bitter flavor), then put it in a saucepan with 1½ cups water. Bring it to a boil, then turn heat to low and let simmer for 12–15 minutes. Remove from heat and set aside to cool.

3. Combine quinoa, black beans, onion, tomatoes, carrot, and cilantro. Stir to combine.

4. Toss salad with ¼ cup of the Tapatio vinaigrette. Taste and adjust seasoning to your liking, adding more dressing, cumin, salt or pepper as needed.

Quinoa

Quinoa (pronounced "keen-WAH") is a plant that has been cultivated in the Andes mountains of South America since 3000 B.C. Ancient Incas called quinoa "the mother grain." It has a nutty flavor and varieties come in colors ranging from tan to red to black. Quinoa is growing in popularity, likely because it is highly nutritious. It can be used as a substitute for grains like rice, but contains high amounts of fiber.

8 ounces small elbow macaroni

1¼ cups half and half

½ yellow onion, finely diced

3 teaspoons hot sauce of your choosing

2 cups grated Cheddar cheese

1½ tablespoons all-purpose flour

½ cup plain bread crumbs

½ teaspoon cayenne pepper

Spicy Mac and Cheese

Any Mexican-style hot sauce such as Tapatio, Valentina, or Cholula would be a good choice for this recipe.

1. Cook macaroni in boiling salted water until just short of done. (Noodles should be *al dente*— slightly chewy.)

2. Heat oven to 400°F. Butter a 9" x 13" baking dish.

3. Bring half and half, onion, and hot sauce to a simmer in a large saucepan over medium heat.

4. Toss Cheddar cheese and flour together in a bowl so cheese is mostly coated; add mixture to half and half. Whisk until sauce is smooth. Return sauce to simmer and let cook another 2–3 minutes.

5. Add pasta to sauce and stir to combine.

6. Spread pasta mixture into baking dish.

7. Toss bread crumbs with cayenne pepper in a small bowl. Sprinkle on top of pasta.

8. Bake mac and cheese until heated through and bread crumbs begin to brown, about 20–30 minutes.

1 (5-ounce) can drained crab meat

1 (8-ounce) package softened cream cheese

3 tablespoons heavy whipping cream

2 teaspoons diced onion

2 teaspoons diced red pepper

2 teaspoons diced jalapeño pepper

2 teaspoons diced tomato

2 teaspoons diced green onion

2 teaspoons white wine

1 tablespoon Parmesan cheese

½ teaspoon Old Bay seasoning

Tabasco sauce, to taste

Spicy Crab Dip

Who doesn't love a good crab dip, and the spicier the better.

1. In a small microwave-safe dish, combine all the ingredients.

2. Microwave on medium power for 4 minutes.

3. Remove from microwave, stir, and serve with bread or chips.

3 sticks of softened butter

½ cup Tabasco sauce

3 tablespoons brown sugar

2 tablespoons chili sauce

1 tablespoon balsamic vinegar

¾ teaspoon salt

¾ teaspoon paprika

⅜ teaspoon cayenne pepper

Tabasco Hot Wing Sauce

A classic hot wing sauce using the classic Louisiana hot sauce.

1. Mix all the ingredients together.

2. Store in the refrigerator for up to 2 weeks.

3 cups flour

2½ teaspoons salt

1 teaspoon paprika

¼ teaspoon cayenne pepper

5 pound bag of chicken wings

1 recipe Tabasco Hot Wing Sauce (see recipe in this chapter)

Tabasco Hot Wings

This recipe makes a big batch for a crowd, which would be a great addition to any party.

1. In a large mixing bowl, combine flour and spices.

2. Cut chicken into wings and drumettes. Wash and allow to drain.

3. Coat the wings with flour mixture and refrigerate for 90 minutes.

4. Preheat a deep fryer to 350°F.

5. Fry wings in hot oil for 8–10 minutes until golden brown. Do not crowd the wings, and fry in batches.

6. Place the wings on paper towels to remove excess oil.

7. When all the wings are fried, place in a large bowl.

8. Add the Tabasco Hot Wing Sauce and mix completely.

CHAPTER 10

Spice Mixes and Dry Rubs

4 ancho chilies, stemmed, seeded, and roughly chopped

4–5 chiles de arbol, stemmed and seeded

2 tablespoons ground cumin

2 tablespoons garlic powder

1 tablespoon dried oregano

1 teaspoon paprika (hot or sweet)

½ teaspoon cayenne pepper

Homemade Chili Powder

Of course you can go to any store and buy chili powder in a bottle, but where's the fun in that? Making your own is easy and, best of all, you can customize it however you like. Here's a basic recipe, but feel free to tinker with it and add more heat or use different types of chilies.

1. Lightly toast the chilies on a comal or cast iron skillet until they puff slightly.

2. Put chilies in a food processor or blender and blend until they form a fine powder. Transfer to a bowl.

3. Add the remaining ingredients and stir well until thoroughly mixed.

4. Store in an airtight container for up to 6 months.

Origins of Chili Powder

No one knows the exact origins of chili powder, but the original version of what you see in supermarkets was created in the United States sometime in the nineteenth century. Chili powder was developed as the way to flavor Southwestern-staple chili con carne. For every household that made chili, there was likely a unique chili powder blend.

1 teaspoon fenugreek seeds

½ cup dried red chilies such as Japone or chiles de arbol, ground

½ cup hot paprika

2 tablespoons salt

1 teaspoon ground ginger

2 teaspoons onion powder

1 teaspoon ground green cardamom

1 teaspoon ground nutmeg

1 teaspoon garlic powder

¼ teaspoon ground cloves

½ teaspoon ground cinnamon

¼ teaspoon ground allspice

Berbere

This complex, heady spice mix is the foundation for all Ethiopian cooking. There are a lot of ingredients, but it's well worth all the grinding and mixing. Try to use whole spices as much as possible and feel free to adjust seasoning to your liking.

1. Grind all the whole spices in a spice or coffee grinder. Be careful not to inhale all the bits of spice that will be released during the process.

2. Pour all the spices into a bowl and stir well until completely combined.

3. Store in an airtight container in the refrigerator for up to 3 months.

Berbere

In Ethiopia, the process of making berbere can take days—even up to 1 week. Chilies are often dried in the sun for multiple days, then ground by hand with a mortar and pestle. Then the chilies are combined with other spices and left to dry in the sun again. While the fundamental flavors are the same, families each have its own unique berbere recipe and mix.

Creole Seasoning Blend

INGREDIENTS | YIELDS ABOUT 1 CUP

5 tablespoons hot paprika

3 tablespoons kosher salt

2 tablespoons garlic powder

2 tablespoons onion powder

2 tablespoons dried oregano

2 tablespoons dried basil

2 tablespoons black pepper

1 tablespoon dried thyme

1 tablespoon cayenne pepper

1 tablespoon white pepper

The building block for so many great Southern dishes like gumbo and jambalaya, this spice blend also works great as a rub for barbecue chicken and shrimp.

1. Combine all ingredients in a bowl and stir well.

2. Store in an airtight container for up to 6 months.

6 tablespoons kosher salt

6 tablespoons granulated garlic

2 tablespoons ground black pepper

2 tablespoons onion powder

2 tablespoons ground cumin

2 tablespoons ground coriander

2 tablespoons chili powder (a smoky, chipotle powder would be good, but use whatever you have on hand)

¼ teaspoon allspice

½ teaspoon dried oregano

Adobo Seasoning

Adobo is a spice mixture that is used throughout Latin America and the Caribbean. Try it on pork, chicken, or fish—then grill, roast, or fry.

1. Put all ingredients in a bowl and stir until thoroughly combined.

2. Store in an airtight container for up to a year.

6 tablespoons ground coriander

4 tablespoons ground cumin

2 tablespoons black pepper

2 tablespoons ground cinnamon

1 tablespoon turmeric

1 tablespoon ground ginger

1 tablespoon cayenne pepper

1 teaspoon ground nutmeg

1 teaspoon ground cloves

Curry Powder

This basic curry powder recipe, which you should take and customize to your own liking, will give you a new appreciation for this complex spice mix that adds flavor to so many dishes. Use ground spices or grind your own.

1. Grind whatever spices need grinding.

2. Combine all ingredients and stir until well combined.

3. Store in airtight container for up to 6 months.

Turmeric

Turmeric is the spice that gives all curry powder its distinct yellow-orange hue. Turmeric has an astringent yet earthy flavor, akin to mustard or horseradish, but more mellow. Its strong color will dye any food that it is sprinkled on. You might also find fresh turmeric at specialty grocery stores, where it looks similar to its cousin, ginger root.

1 teaspoon ground cloves

1 teaspoon ground ginger

1 teaspoon ground cardamom

1 teaspoon ground mace

1 teaspoon ground nutmeg

1 teaspoon ground black pepper

1 teaspoon ground cinnamon

1 teaspoon ground allspice

1 teaspoon ground turmeric

1 teaspoon hot paprika

Ras Al Hanout

In Arabic, Ras Al Hanout *means "top of the shop" and refers to a spice owner's special blend of his best spices. It's an essential Moroccan spice mix and some versions have upward of 20 or even 30 ingredients. Try it rubbed on lamb or beef.*

1. Combine all the spices and stir until thoroughly mixed.

2. Store in an airtight container for up to 6 months.

2 tablespoons ground black peppercorns

2 tablespoons hot paprika

1 tablespoon ground coriander seeds

1 tablespoon ground cumin

1 tablespoon ground cloves

1 tablespoon ground mint

2 teaspoons ground nutmeg

1 teaspoon ground cinnamon

Baharat

Baharat is a spice mix used throughout the Middle East: Lebanon, Syria, Israel, Jordan. Its name simply means spice *in Arabic. There are endless variations, so feel free to experiment. Try Baharat on different meats and vegetables, or stirred into rice pilaf.*

1. Combine all spices and mix well.

2. Store in airtight container for up to 6 months.

2 dried chipotle peppers

2 dried ancho chili peppers

1 teaspoon cayenne pepper

2 tablespoons brown sugar

1 teaspoon salt

½ teaspoon garlic pepper

Three-Chili Rub

Use this recipe as a substitute for any ground chili powder, and use it as a dry rub for grilled, barbecued, and smoked meats.

1. In small heavy skillet, toast chipotle peppers until fragrant, stirring frequently; remove to a kitchen towel to let cool.

2. Toast the ancho peppers in same skillet until fragrant and let cool on kitchen towel. Remove stems and grind the cooled chilies in a spice grinder.

3. Combine with remaining ingredients and mix well.

4. Store in an airtight container for up to 6 months.

1 tablespoon whole cumin

¼ cup sweet paprika

2 tablespoons chili powder

2 tablespoons packed dark brown sugar

1 tablespoon granulated sugar

1 tablespoon ground black pepper

1 teaspoon cayenne pepper

1 tablespoon minced garlic mashed to a paste with 1 tablespoon salt

Memphis Dry Rub

This is an ideal dry rub for barbecue pork ribs: sweet, smoky, and definitely spicy.

1. In a small skillet over medium-high heat, toast cumin until it is fragrant, 1–2 minutes. Remove and let cool. Grind to a fine powder in a spice or coffee grinder.

2. Transfer cumin to a small bowl. Combine with the rest of the ingredients.

3. Mix ingredients well; be sure that the garlic is completely incorporated.

4. Use immediately.

Making a Garlic Paste

Garlic paste with salt is an easy, quick way to add flavor to your food. Mince garlic on your cutting board, then sprinkle a little salt over it. Working at an angle, move the edge of the knife back and forth across the garlic until it's smooth. The pressure from your knife, along with the salt grains, breaks the garlic down into a flavorful paste.

1 tablespoon ancho chili powder

1 guajillo chili, stemmed, seeded, and roughly chopped

1 tablespoon ground cumin

1 tablespoon light brown sugar

1 teaspoon kosher salt

½ teaspoon ground cinnamon

½ teaspoon ground black pepper

Ancho and Guajillo Chili Dry Rub

This dry rub gets an extra hit of sweet heat from the guajillo chilies. This is perfect on pork chops.

1. Combine all the ingredients in a food processor or spice grinder. Grind into a fine powder.

2. Use immediately.

¾ cup paprika

¼ cup ground black pepper

¼ cup salt

¼ cup light brown sugar

¼ cup unsweetened cocoa powder

2 tablespoons chili powder

2 tablespoons garlic powder

1 tablespoon cayenne pepper

Cocoa and Chili Dry Rub

Here's an unexpected twist on a spicy dry rub. It might not make sense at first, but the cocoa powder adds a nice warmth and depth to the mix.

1. Combine all ingredients in a bowl and mix well.

2. Store in an airtight container for up to 6 months.

Cocoa Powder

Cocoa powder is made when chocolate liquor (not the alcoholic liqueur, but chocolate in its pure, liquid form) is squeezed to remove the cocoa butter. The solid that's left behind is processed into a powder, which carries the chocolate flavor before being sweetened. Besides baking, cocoa powder can be used in savory applications.

CHAPTER 11

The Heat Capital: Mexico

2 dried pasilla or New Mexico chilies

2 dried guajillo chilies

2 cups water, brought to a boil

2 teaspoons dried oregano

1½ teaspoons salt

½ teaspoon cumin seeds

2 garlic cloves, peeled and lightly smashed

1 tomato, roughly chopped

1 white onion, roughly chopped

2 pounds pork shoulder (boneless or not) or country-style pork ribs, cut into 1" cubes

2 (15-ounce) cans of white hominy, drained and rinsed

Red Pork and Hominy Stew

This hearty stew, called posole rojo, *has infinite variations across Mexico. This recipe gets richer flavor from two kinds of dried chilies. Feel free to experiment with different chilies you may have at home. Like all soups, it tastes even better after a day or two.*

1. Remove the seeds and stems from the dried chilies. Place in a bowl and cover with boiling water. Let sit until softened, about 15 minutes.

2. Transfer the chilies and soaking water to a blender. Add the oregano, salt, cumin, garlic, tomato and onion, then blend until smooth. (Use caution as hot liquids expand in the blender.)

3. Transfer the chili purée to a 4-quart heavy saucepan, add the pork, and bring to a boil. Reduce heat, cover and simmer until pork is tender, about 1 hour.

4. Add the hominy, stir, and simmer covered for another 20–30 minutes. Skim fat from surface and season to taste with salt and pepper. Thin broth with water if you like.

5. Serve in bowls with toppings such as diced onion, cabbage, and lime wedges.

Hominy

While there are many different recipes for *posole* (pork), they all have one ingredient in common: hominy. Hominy, a staple of Native Americans in both North and South America, are dried white or yellow corn kerns from which the hulls have been removed. Kernels are treated with an alkali in a process called *nixtamalization*, after which it is easier for the hull to be taken off and for the hominy to be used in cooking.

2 pounds pork shoulder or country-style ribs, cut into 1" squares

4 cups water, or meat stock of your choice

1 white onion, roughly chopped

1 bay leaf

2 teaspoons dried oregano

2 teaspoons kosher salt

Ground black pepper, to taste

2 garlic cloves, peeled and roughly chopped

2 (15-ounce) cans of hominy, drained and rinsed

2 serrano chilies, with seeds, finely chopped

2 limes, cut into wedges

4 springs of cilantro, finely chopped

¼ cup raw cabbage, finely chopped (optional)

White Pork and Hominy Stew

This posole blanco *(white posole) is a simpler, cleaner version of the Red Pork and Hominy Stew (see recipe in this chapter), but no less tasty. Garnish this version with plenty of chopped fresh serrano, lime, and cilantro. Using on-the-bone pork meat will make the broth richer.*

1. Combine the pork, water, onion, bay leaf, oregano, salt, pepper, and garlic in a 4-quart heavy sauce pan. Bring to a boil, then reduce heat and simmer for 45 minutes, until pork is softened and tender.

2. Add the hominy, bring to boil again, then reduce heat and let simmer for another 20 minutes.

3. Serve in bowls and garnish as you like with serrano, lime, cilantro, and cabbage.

4 ears of corn, shucked and boiled or grilled

¼ cup unsalted butter, softened

¼ cup mayonnaise

½ cup grated Cotija or Parmesan cheese

1 teaspoon chili powder

1 lime, cut into wedges

Salt, to taste

Elotes

This Mexican version of corn on the cob, a popular street food, is downright addictive: spicy, tangy, smoky, and sweet. Add as little or as much chili powder as you like. Boiled corn works fine, but grilling will give it extra flavor.

1. Remove cooked corn from the water or off the grill. Pat dry to get rid of any excess water.

2. Mix the softened butter with the mayonnaise and spread mixture over the corn cobs.

3. Sprinkle the corn with chili powder and grated cheese. Squirt lime over corn. Season to taste with salt.

Cotija Cheese

Cotija cheese is a hard cheese made from cow's milk that is found all over Mexico. It is dry and firm, crumbles easily, and has a delightfully salty flavor. If you can't find Cotija, you can substitute it with Parmesan. In fact, many street vendors in Mexico use the American standard Kraft Parmesan cheese from the green shaker.

2 pounds bone-in chicken breasts

1 teaspoon salt

4 cloves garlic, roughly chopped

1 pound tomatillos, husked and washed

2 serrano chilies, seeded, finely chopped

¼ cup loosely packed fresh cilantro, roughly chopped

2 teaspoons vegetable oil

8 corn tortillas (6" in diameter)

2 cups Monterey jack cheese, shredded

Enchiladas Suizas

This recipe includes the steps for making a quick, tangy green salsa. However, if you've got extra green salsa around (or a favorite jarred green salsa), feel free to skip making the sauce from scratch.

1. Place chicken breasts in a large saucepan and cover with water. Add 1 teaspoon of salt and 2 garlic cloves. Bring to a boil, then reduce heat, cover, and simmer for 15–20 minutes. Remove chicken and let cool.

2. When chicken is cool enough to handle, remove skin and pull meat from bones. Shred and set aside.

3. Place tomatillos and chilies in a saucepan and cover with water (you could also use the leftover broth you poached the chicken in). Boil over medium-high heat for 6–8 minutes. Transfer to a blender, along with remaining garlic and cilantro. Blend until smooth, adding liquid if necessary.

4. Heat oil in a small saucepan over medium-high heat. Add tomatillo sauce and reduce heat to medium. Simmer, stirring constantly, 10 minutes or until sauce reduces and thickens.

5. Heat oven to 350°F. Heat a skillet over medium heat; warm tortillas for about 10 seconds per side. Divide shredded chicken evenly among tortillas along with a spoonful of sauce; roll up.

6. Spread about ⅓ of the sauce in the bottom of a 9" x 13" baking dish. Arrange enchiladas in one layer, folded side down. Cover with the rest of sauce and sprinkle with cheese.

7. Bake enchiladas for 30 minutes or until cheese starts to bubble and brown. Serve immediately.

2 large nopal (cactus) pads, available at Mexican or specialty grocery stores

½ large white onion, diced

2 medium tomatoes, cubed

4 sprigs fresh cilantro leaves, finely chopped

2 jalapeño peppers, seeded, and finely chopped

1 avocado, peeled, pitted, and cubed (optional)

Juice of 1 lime

Salt and pepper, to taste

Cactus Salad

Cactus leaves, called nopales, *are a common salad ingredient in Mexico. They have a distinct crunch and texture similar to okra. If you're not sure about handling fresh nopales, you can also buy them jarred at most Mexican groceries.*

1. Clean the nopales with a vegetable peeler or small paring knife. Using caution, remove all the thorns and bumps, paying special attention to the edges of the pads.

2. Cut the nopales into bite-sized pieces and boil in water with a bit of salt for 25 minutes or until tender. Drain well.

3. Put nopales in a large bowl. Add all remaining ingredients then stir gently until thoroughly mixed.

4. Put in the refrigerator until salad is cooled.

¾ cup long-grain white rice

2 ancho chilies, seeds and ribs removed

1 cup water or chicken broth

3 tablespoons vegetable oil

¼ cup finely chopped white onion

Salt, to taste

Rice Cooked with Ancho Chili

Try this as a side dish for grilled or roasted meats for a mild but still spicy side dish.

1. Put the rice in a bowl and cover with hot water for 5 minutes. Rinse well and set aside to drain.

2. Lightly toast the anchos on a comal or cast iron skillet for a few seconds on each side (careful not to burn them or they will get bitter). Put in a bowl and cover with hot water or chicken broth and let soak until softened, about 15 minutes. Remove from water and cut into thin strips. Save the soaking liquid.

3. Heat the oil in a heavy-bottomed saucepan or deep skillet. Add the dry rice and stir until all the grains have been coated in a bit of oil. Add the onion and continue frying over medium heat until the rice starts to brown lightly, about 5 minutes.

4. Add the water, ancho chilies, salt, and ½ cup of the soaking liquid to the rice. Cook, covered, on low heat until all the liquid has been absorbed, about 12–15 minutes.

5. Take off heat, set aside and leave covered for a few minutes. Give the rice a stir to fluff it up before serving.

1 cup long-grain rice

¼ cup vegetable oil

½ white onion, roughly chopped

2 garlic cloves, peeled and roughly chopped

4 jalapeño chilies

4 tomatillos

1¼ cups water or chicken broth, separated

Salt, to taste

Leaves from 4 cilantro leaves, finely chopped

Spicy Green Rice

Another nice way to introduce a bit of spice into a meal is through a side dish. Serve this alongside grilled chicken or fish.

1. Cover the rice with hot water and let soak for 5 minutes. Rinse well and set to drain.

2. Heat the oil in a heavy-bottomed saucepan or deep skillet. Add the dry rice and stir until all the grains have been coated in a bit of oil. Add the onion and 1 clove of garlic and continue frying over medium heat until the rice starts to brown lightly, about 5 minutes.

3. Purée the chilies, tomatillos, and garlic clove with ¼ cup of the water in a blender. Stir the mixture into the rice and fry for a few minutes more, stirring to prevent burning, until the moisture has been mostly absorbed.

4. Add the remaining water, salt, and cilantro and cook over medium heat until all the liquid has been absorbed, about 12–15 minutes.

5. Take off heat, set side and leave covered for a few minutes. Give the rice a stir to fluff it up before serving.

INGREDIENTS | SERVES 6

2 pounds pork, good for stewing, such as country-style ribs or pork shoulder, cut into 1" cubes

6 garlic cloves, roughly chopped

Salt and pepper to taste

1 pound tomatoes

3 tomatillos, husked and washed

3 serrano chilies

4 poblano chilies, roasted, peeled, seeds and ribs removed, cut into thin strips (*rajas*)

Pork with Rajas

This is a relatively simple, one-pot stew that packs a lot of heat and flavor. Serve with warm tortillas for a comforting meal.

1. Put the pork into a deep saucepan or Dutch oven and cover with water. Add garlic, salt, and pepper, cover and bring to a boil. Reduce heat to medium, cover, and let simmer for 15 minutes.

2. Add the tomatoes, tomatillos, and chilies to the pot and continue cooking until the chilies are soft, about 10 minutes. Carefully fish out the vegetables and chilies and place in a blender, along with 1 cup of broth from the pot. Blend until smooth.

3. Take the lid off the pot and continue cooking the pork until it is tender, another 15 minutes. Set aside another cup of broth.

4. Pour off any excess liquid and continue cooking the pork over low heat, until it begins to brown lightly. (You may need to add a touch of oil to do this.)

5. Pour the blended sauce back into the pot and fry over medium-high heat, stirring and scraping the bottom of the pan to prevent sticking, for about 5 minutes.

6. Add the rajas and reserved broth and let simmer until rajas are heated through, about 2–4 minutes. Serve.

Rajas

Rajas are narrow strips of chilies, usually poblanos, that have been roasted. They add a subtle heat and nice flavor to many dishes.

3 tablespoons vegetable oil

1 cup white onions, thinly sliced

Salt and pepper, to taste

6 poblano or Anaheim chilies, roasted, peeled, seeded, and cut into thin strips (*rajas*)

1 cup strong beer (no Corona here, use a darker lager)

¾ cup medium Cheddar cheese, shredded

Rajas Cooked in Beer

Who wouldn't love chili peppers cooked in beer and smothered with cheese? This is a Holy Trinity for many and a guaranteed crowd pleaser.

1. Heat the oil in a skillet. Add the onion, salt and pepper, and cook over low-medium heat until the onions turn soft and translucent, about 3–4 minutes.

2. Add the rajas, stir, cover the pan, and continue to cook until the chilies are tender.

3. Add the beer and continue cooking, uncovered, until it has been absorbed by the rajas.

4. Turn the heat to low, spread the cheese on top, cover and cook until cheese is heated through and melted, about 3 minutes. Serve immediately.

2 tablespoons vegetable oil

8 corn tortillas, each cut into eight triangles

½ onion, roughly chopped

Salt, to taste

½–1 cup of your favorite salsa

Handful of crumbled queso fresco or Cotija cheese

Chilaquiles

Chilaquiles are a great, easy way to use up extra salsa and tortillas you might have around the house. Add a couple of fried eggs on top for a savory breakfast.

1. Heat the oil in skillet. Add the tortilla pieces and fry until they start to turn light brown. Add the onions and salt and keep frying 3–4 minutes long, until the onions are soft and beginning to brown.

2. Turn the heat down and add the salsa. Stir well so that all the tortillas soak up some of the salsa. Continue cooking until salsa is heated through, about 1–2 minutes.

3. Transfer chilaquiles to a plate and top with cheese and toppings of your choice.

Chilaquiles

The term *chilaquiles* translates to "broken up old sombrero," but in actuality it's a way of using up old, stale tortillas. Nearly every region in Mexico has its own version of chilaquiles, some with meat, some with creamy cheese toppings. Pretty much anything goes with this dish, so long as you start with tortillas and salsa. Use up leftovers from your refrigerator—you really can't go wrong.

12 Anaheim or poblano chilies, charred and peeled

1 pound mild, melting cheese like Cheddar or Monterey jack, cut into strips

1 cup milk

1 cup all-purpose flour

1 egg, beaten

1 teaspoon baking powder

1 teaspoon baking soda

1 teaspoon salt

2–3 cups canola oil, for frying

½ cup all-purpose flour for coating

Chiles Rellenos

These battered and fried chilies stuffed with cheese are a guaranteed favorite. To prep the chilies, simply blister them under the broiler for a few minutes on each side, then remove stems, seeds, and skin.

1. Stuff each pepper with a strip of cheese. Set aside.

2. In a small bowl, combine milk, 1 cup of flour, egg, baking powder, baking soda, salt, and canola oil. Mix well to make a batter.

3. Fill a heavy frying pan with about 1" of oil and heat over medium-high heat.

4. Spread the ½ cup of flour on a plate. When oil is hot, dust each stuffed chili in the flour, then dip in the egg batter. Gently drop chilies in oil.

5. Fry chilies until lightly browned on both sides. Remove to a plate covered with a paper towel to absorb excess oil.

Chalupas

INGREDIENTS | SERVES 4

Vegetable oil, for frying

8 small corn tortillas

2 cups of your salsa of choice

1 onion, finely chopped

2 cups shredded chicken or beef (optional)

Shredded cheese such as Monterey Jack, Cheddar, or crumbled queso fresco (optional)

These make a great, quick snack and are an easy way to use up leftover salsa or roasted chicken. Use your favorite homemade salsa or, if you prefer, salsa from a jar.

1. Heat oil in a skillet. Place tortillas in pan and fry until they begin to crisp. Flip the tortillas.

2. With the tortillas still in the pan, add a heaping tablespoon of salsa, some minced onion, as well as shredded meat and/or cheese.

3. Turn the heat to low, cover, and let chalupas cook until toppings are heated through and cheese is melted. Serve.

Chalupas

Chalupas, or *little boats*, are another Mexican staple that has endless variations, depending on the region. Typically, though, they are small tortillas that are loaded with salsa and toppings like vegetables, meat, and cheese, to make a light snack. Chalupa toppings are limited only by your imagination.

4 dried guajillo chilies

2 teaspoons whole cumin seeds

4 whole cloves

½ teaspoon ancho chili powder

1 large onion, roughly chopped

4 cloves garlic, peeled

2 teaspoons dried oregano

1 teaspoon ground thyme

⅓ cup apple cider vinegar

2 teaspoons lime juice

1 (6-pound) boneless beef chuck roast

Barbacoa

Traditional Mexican barbacoa *("barbecue") usually involves lamb or goat, but this recipe calls for beef chuck roast. After slow roasting in the oven for six hours, you won't really care what's in it, you'll just know that it is delicious.*

1. Lightly toast the guajillos in a comal or cast iron skillet until they puff up slightly, about 5 minutes. Remove and set them aside to cool.

2. In the same skillet, toast the cumin seeds and cloves until they are fragrant and seeds begin to pop. Remove and set aside.

3. When the chilies are cool enough to handle, remove the stems, seeds, and ribs. Place in a bowl, cover with boiling water, and let the chilies soak until soft, at least 15 minutes.

4. Grind the toasted cumin and cloves in spice or coffee grinder and put in a blender. Add chili powder, onion, garlic, oregano, thyme, vinegar, and lime juice. Add the guajillo chilies, along with ¼ cup of the soaking liquid. Blend into a smooth paste.

5. Rinse the beef roast and pat dry. Place in a large mixing bowl and pour the guajillo paste over it. Using your hands, spread the paste on all sides of the roast. Cover the bowl with plastic wrap and put in the refrigerator to marinate at least 2 hours. (The longer you let it marinate, the better. If you have time, let it sit overnight.)

A History of Barbecue

The term *barbecue* originates with the indigenous Taino people of the Caribbean, whose word *barabicu* described their technique of slow-roasting animals in a pit. Typically, turkey and fish were rubbed with spice pastes and left to cook for many hours underground. When the Spanish introduced pigs, goats, and chickens, barbecue grew to include these meats well. Obviously, the tradition is alive and well today, all over the world.

6. Take the roast out of the refrigerator and let it come to room temperature. Preheat an oven to 325°F.

7. Put the roast in a roasting pan and cover tightly with aluminum foil. Bake the roast in the oven until the meat is fall-apart tender, about 6 hours.

8. When roast is done, take it out of the oven and let it stand, covered, at room temperature for about 1 hour before shredding the meat with a fork.

9. Serve the meat, with its juices, as tacos or as an entrée with rice and tortillas.

1 pound medium shrimp, still in shells

1 cup fresh lime juice

½ cup fresh lemon juice

1 small red onion, finely chopped

1 serrano chili, finely chopped (for less heat, remove seeds and ribs)

1 cup cilantro leaves, finely chopped

1 avocado, peeled, pitted, and cut into small chunks

Salt and pepper, to taste

Shrimp Ceviche

Ceviche is a Latin American technique of "cooking" seafood by marinating it in citrus juice. In this recipe, you parboil the shrimp first for safety since shellfish is especially prone to bacteria.

1. Fill a large bowl with ice water and set aside. Fill a large pot with water, salt it generously, and bring to a boil. Add the shrimp and cook for 1–2 minutes, until just pink.

2. Remove shrimp and immediately place in bowl of ice water to stop cooking. (If the shrimp is overcooked, it will be rubbery instead of soft.)

3. Drain the shrimp. Peel and devein shrimp, then slice into small chunks. Place shrimp in a nonreactive (glass or ceramic) bowl.

4. Add the lemon and lime juice. Cover and refrigerate for 15–30 minutes.

5. Add the red onion and serrano. Cover and refrigerate for another 30 minutes.

6. Just before serving, add the cilantro and avocado. Season with salt and pepper to taste. Serve with tortilla chips or tostadas.

Salt and pepper, to taste

1 (3-pound) pork shoulder roast

2–3 tablespoons olive oil

1 thinly sliced onion

4 medium tomatoes

½ teaspoon dried oregano

1 teaspoon cumin powder

2 bay leaves

2 whole cloves

2 dried chipotle chilies

¾ cup water or meat stock

Pork Carnitas

Mexican pork carnitas are slow-cooked, shredded pork shoulder usually served with tortillas and salsa. The chipotle peppers give this recipe great flavor, but if you need more heat, add a dash of your favorite hot sauce as well.

1. Preheat the oven to 325°F.

2. Salt and pepper the pork and allow the meat to come to room temperature.

3. Add olive oil to a large oven-proof pan.

4. Sear the pork in the pan over medium-high heat for 5 minutes per side.

5. Remove the pork from the pan and let it rest for 10–15 minutes.

6. Add onions and cook over low heat for 2–3 minutes until translucent.

7. Return the pork to the pan and add the remaining ingredients.

8. Cover and place in the oven. Cook for 2–3 hours, until the internal temperature reaches 140°F–150°F.

9. Let the roast rest for 10–15 minutes before slicing.

CHAPTER 12

From Texas Chili to Chimichurri: The Americas

10 jalapeño peppers

8 ounces cream cheese, brought to room temperature

½ cup goat cheese, brought to room temperature

2 tablespoons cilantro, finely chopped

2 garlic cloves, finely chopped

½ teaspoon salt

Pinch of cayenne pepper

Black pepper, to taste

Juice of half a lemon

Jalapeño Poppers

These peppers aren't the deep-fried versions you'll find at bars, but they're just as gooey, cheesy, and tasty.

1. Heat the oven to 450°F and position an oven rack in the middle.

2. Slice jalapeños lengthwise down the center. Remove the seeds and ribs from inside the peppers and discard.

3. Combine cream cheese, goat cheese, cilantro, garlic, salt, cayenne, black pepper, and lemon juice in a medium bowl. Stir until all ingredients are smooth thoroughly mixed.

4. Spoon the cheese mixture into each of the jalapeño halves. Place the filled peppers on a greased baking sheet about 2" apart.

5. Bake until the peppers are starting to char and the filling is browned and bubbly, about 12–15 minutes. Remove from the oven and let cool for 5 minutes before serving.

INGREDIENTS | SERVES 6–8

⅓ cup flour

2 pounds beef shoulder, cut into ½" cubes

1 pound pork shoulder, cut into ½" cubes

⅓ cup bacon fat (you can use vegetable oil if you don't have any bacon fat on hand)

2 large onions, diced

6 cloves garlic, minced

1½ cups chicken or beef broth

4 cups water

4 dried ancho chili peppers

3 dried New Mexico chili peppers

3 dried serrano chili peppers

2 teaspoons cumin

1 teaspoon dried Mexican oregano

San Antonio Beef Chili

Long before Texas became a U.S. state, the "Chili Queens" of San Antonio would sell their chilies from outdoor kettles in the public square.

1. Toss flour with beef and pork until meat is lightly coated. In a large, heavy saucepan or Dutch oven, heat bacon fat over medium-high heat. Brown beef and pork; add onions and garlic. Cook 2–3 minutes, or until onions soften.

2. Add broth; stir well. Lower heat to medium; simmer 20 minutes, stirring often.

3. Add 2 cups water. While meat mixture continues to simmer, remove stems and seeds from dried peppers. Cut peppers into pieces; place in a heat-safe bowl. Bring remaining 2 cups water to a boil; pour over chilies. Let stand 20 minutes.

4. Remove chilies from water with slotted spoon; place in food processor or blender with small amount of soaking water. Pulse to purée; add to simmering meat.

5. Add cumin and oregano; stir well. Simmer uncovered 2 hours. Stir often; add water if chili becomes too dry.

A Bowl of Red

Chili lovers are often surprised to learn that the famous southern Texas Bowl of Red is often made without tomatoes, and beans are always served on the side. Chili champions from the Lone Star State may claim to add any number of secret ingredients to their creations—from coffee grounds to rattlesnake meat—but the rich red sauce color comes from sun-ripened chili peppers.

2 teaspoons vegetable oil

¾ pound pork stew meat, cut into 1" chunks

3 garlic cloves, peeled and finely chopped

1 onion, finely chopped

1 jalapeño pepper, finely chopped

1 (28-ounce) can of roasted New Mexican green chilies, roughly chopped or torn apart by hand

1 teaspoon cumin

Salt and black pepper, to taste

3 cups chicken broth

New Mexico Green Chili Stew

For best results, use authentic New Mexican chilies. If you can't find them at the store, order them at The Hatch Chili Express: www.hatch-chile.com.

1. Heat oil in a large Dutch oven. Add pork and brown on all sides, about 5 minutes.

2. Add garlic, onion, and jalapeño, and stir. Cook until onion and garlic soften and become translucent, about 5 minutes more.

3. Add chilies, spices, and chicken broth. Bring mixture to a boil, then lower heat and let simmer until pork is tender, at least 1 hour.

4. If you have time, let stew simmer on very low for 2–4 hours. Add a little liquid if it becomes too thick.

3 cups all-purpose flour

1 cup yellow cornmeal

⅛ cup sugar

2 tablespoons baking powder

2 tablespoons salt

2 cups milk

3 large eggs, lightly beaten

½ pound (2 sticks) unsalted butter, melted, and cooled

2⅔ cups Cheddar cheese (mild or sharp, it's up to you), grated

1 bunch scallions, both white and green parts, chopped

2 jalapeño peppers, finely chopped (you can seed the peppers for less heat)

Jalapeño and Cheddar Cornbread

Sweet, savory, and spicy all at once. Serve this with chili for a hearty meal.

1. In a large bowl, combine the flour, cornmeal, sugar, baking powder, and salt.

2. In smaller bowl, combine milk, eggs, and butter.

3. Add the wet ingredients to the dry ingredients and stir well, until most of the lumps are gone and batter is smooth.

4. Add ⅔ of the grated cheese, plus the scallions and jalapeños. Let the batter sit at room temperature for 15 minutes.

5. Heat the oven to 350°F. Grease a 9" × 13" baking pan. Mix in 2 cups of the grated Cheddar, scallions, and jalapeños, and allow the mixture to sit at room temperature for 20 minutes.

6. Pour the batter into the pan and shake gently so it spreads evenly. Sprinkle the remaining cheese on top. Bake for 30–35 minutes, until a knife or toothpick stuck into the center comes out clean.

Baking Powder versus Baking Soda

Both baking powder and baking soda are leavening agents, which means they are added to baked goods to make them rise. Baking soda is pure sodium bicarbonate, while baking powder is sodium bicarbonate along with an acidifying agent and a starch. Recipes that use baking powder often call for more neutral-tasting ingredients; baking powder is a common ingredient in cakes and biscuits.

1 tablespoon vegetable oil

1 pound andouille sausage, sliced

1 large onion, diced

1 rib celery, diced

1 bell pepper, cored and diced

2 garlic cloves, peeled and minced

½ pound diced ham (tasso or smoked, if you have it)

1 pound chicken meat, cut into chunks

2 pounds shrimp, peeled and deveined

1 (14-ounce) can diced tomatoes

3 (14-ounce) cans tomato sauce

2 teaspoons chicken broth

1 teaspoon Tabasco sauce, or more to taste

2 bay leaves

1 teaspoon dried sage

½ teaspoon dried thyme leaves

⅓ cup sliced green onions

⅓ cup minced fresh parsley

Salt and pepper, to taste

Cajun Jambalaya

Don't let the length of the ingredients list deter you. This dish is simple to make and rewards you with layers of bold flavors.

1. In a heavy soup pot over medium-high heat, combine oil and sliced andouille. Sauté, stirring constantly, until sausage begins to brown. Add onion, celery, and bell pepper; continue to sauté 3–5 minutes, until vegetables are crisp-tender.

2. Add garlic, ham, chicken, and shrimp. Stir well to blend; cook 1 minute. Add tomatoes, tomato sauce, broth, Tabasco, bay leaves, sage, and thyme; stir to combine. Bring to a boil.

3. Reduce heat to medium low; cover. Simmer 40 minutes, stirring occasionaly.

4. Remove cover; continue cooking an additional 20 minutes, or until mixture reaches desired thickness.

5. Turn off heat; add green onions, parsley, salt, and pepper. Cover; let stand 5 minutes before serving. Serve over steamed white rice.

Tasso Ham

Tasso ham is a Cajun specialty. It's a heavily smoked piece of pork that is extra peppery and spicy, thanks to a rub with lots of cayenne pepper that is applied before smoking. Tasso provides a flavor base for many dishes, from soups and stews to braised vegetables and gravy. If you can't get your hands on tasso, substitute smoked ham.

Oyster Po' Boys

Serve these "dressed" with shredded lettuce, sliced tomatoes, pickles, and onion.

1. Combine cornmeal, flour, salt and pepper, and cayenne.

2. Heat oil in a medium skillet over medium-high heat.

3. Pat each oyster dry with a paper towel. Dip them in the cornmeal crust then lay gently into the skillet.

4. Fry oysters in batches until golden brown, turning once, about 5 minutes total. Set to dry on a plate lined with paper towels to absorb excess oil.

5. Spread rolls with Spicy Remoulade Sauce. Add oysters, then dress with fixings.

Po' Boy History

The po' boy sandwich, a New Orleans tradition, got its name during a streetcar operator strike in 1929. In solidarity with striking workers, a New Orleans restaurant owned by brothers Benny and Cloves Martin offered to feed train conductors for free. When workers would show up for their sandwiches the folks behind the counter would call out, "Here comes another poor boy."

1 rack baby back pork ribs

5 tablespoons Memphis Dry Rub (see Chapter 10)

1–2 cups barbecue sauce (homemade or your favorite bottled)

Oven-Baked Barbecue Ribs

This recipe is for two racks of ribs, but you can easily double, triple, or quadruple the recipe by simply adding more ribs to the foil packet.

1. Heat oven to 225°F. Cover ribs with Memphis Dry Rub and, using your hands, massage dry rub all over.

2. Place rib rack in baking dish, meat side down, and cover tightly with foil. Bake in oven for 3½ hours.

3. Remove ribs from oven. Remove foil, then carefully flip ribs so meat side is up.

4. Slather ribs with barbecue sauce and return to oven, uncovered. Bake for another 20–30 minutes.

4 round, ½-pound loaves of pumpernickel or honey wheat bread

4 boneless chicken breasts

2 tablespoons flour

1 teaspoon salt

½ teaspoon cayenne

1 teaspoon chili powder

½ cup butter

1 small onion, minced

3 jalapeño peppers, minced

2 garlic cloves, minced

2 tablespoons tomato paste

¼ cup white vinegar

¼ cup hot sauce, of your choice

1 teaspoon sugar

1½ cups water or chicken broth

½ cup beer

2 ribs celery, sliced

½ cup sour cream

¼ cup blue cheese dressing

Buffalo Chicken in a Bread Bowl

It's always fun when you can eat both the dinner and plate.

1. Slice tops off bread loaves; set aside. Carefully hollow out insides, leaving at least ½ thick shell. (Reserve bread for bread crumbs.) Place each bread loaf on plate or in shallow bowl.

2. Dice chicken breasts. Combine flour, salt, cayenne, and chili powder; coat chicken in flour mixture. In a large saucepan, melt butter over medium-high heat. Brown chicken in butter; remove to platter. Add onion, jalapeño peppers, and garlic; sauté 3 minutes.

3. Add tomato paste; cook, stirring, 1 minute. Add vinegar, hot sauce, sugar, water or broth, and beer; bring to a boil. Cook 10 minutes, allowing sauce to reduce.

4. Add celery and chicken; reduce heat to medium and continue cooking 10 minutes. Remove from heat; let stand 5 minutes.

5. Spoon hot chicken and celery into bread bowls with some of the sauce. Combine sour cream and dressing; place a dollop over each bread bowl and serve with bread tops on the side.

1 pound Dungeness crabmeat

2 hard-boiled eggs, peeled

2 Roma tomatoes

¼ cup cocktail sauce or ketchup

½ cup mayonnaise

1 tablespoon heavy cream

1 teaspoon Tabasco sauce

1 tablespoon chopped parsley

1 tablespoon minced green bell pepper

1 tablespoon minced green onions

1 teaspoon lemon juice

2 cups shredded iceberg lettuce

Dungeness Crab Louis

San Francisco and Seattle both claim to be the birthplace of Crab Louis. In either case, it is a vintage recipe from the turn of the twentieth century using Pacific coast crabmeat and pink dressing.

1. Pick through the crabmeat to remove any cartilage, then set aside.

2. Cut the eggs and tomatoes into quarters, then set aside.

3. Mix the cocktail sauce, mayonnaise, cream, Tabasco, parsley, bell pepper, green onions, and lemon juice together to make the pink dressing.

4. Divide the lettuce among four plates. Place a mound of crabmeat on each plate of lettuce. Pour the dressing over the crabmeat.

5. Garnish each plate with two wedges of egg and two wedges of tomato.

½ cup Jerk Sauce (see Chapter 6)

3 pounds chicken, either whole or use legs and thighs (bone-in and skin-on)

Jerk Chicken

Jerk is a classic Caribbean preparation. It's most often grilled, but this recipe allows you to do it in the oven.

1. Heat the oven to 350°F.

2. Using your hands, take the Jerk Sauce and rub all over the chicken, both under and on top of the skin.

3. Place the chicken in a baking dish. Roast for 1 hour 15 minutes.

4. Check the chicken with thermometer to be sure juices run clear and that the thickest thigh measures 160°F. Roast longer if necessary.

Jerking

Far from being an insult in Jamaica and throughout the Caribbean, *jerk* refers to a method of cooking meats by rubbing it with a mixture of spices like allspice and cinnamon. Jerk is famously spicy thanks to fiery Scotch bonnet peppers. Most jerk meat is grilled over hardwood charcoal in a steel drum pan.

INGREDIENTS | SERVES 8

½ cup Adobo Seasoning (see Chapter 10)

1 tablespoon apple cider vinegar

1 (4-pound) pork shoulder

Pernil (Puerto Rican Roasted Pork Shoulder)

Once you make this, you'll want to eat it all the time. The pork is done when it's so tender that it collapses at the slightest touch.

1. Heat oven to 300°F.

2. Combine Adobo Seasoning with vinegar to make a thick paste.

3. Score the top of the pork shoulder with a sharp knife in a crosshatch pattern. Using your hands, rub the paste all over and into the pork shoulder, getting into the cuts and every nook and cranny.

4. Put pork in a roasting pan and fill the bottom with a little water. Roast pork for about 3 hours, turning every hour and adding more water as necessary, until meat is very tender.

5. Let meat rest for 10–15 minutes before cutting. The meat should be so tender that it falls apart, so instead of slices it should form big shreds.

Adobo

Depending on what country you are from, *adobo* can mean many different things. In Spain, it's a sauce made from oil, garlic, and marjoram. In Mexico, it means a marinade of guajillo chili, garlic, vinegar, and spices like bay, oregano, and canela. And in the Philippines, it refers to an iconic dish of meat braised in vinegar, soy sauce, garlic, and bay.

4 (1½"-thick) rib eye steaks (2–2½ pounds total)

Salt and pepper

1 tablespoon olive oil

1 cup Chimichurri (see Chapter 6)

Grilled Steak with Chimichurri

Steak for dinner is always a treat, especially with this spicy, tangy Argentinian sauce.

1. Season the steaks all over with plenty of salt and ground black pepper. Heat 1 tablespoon of olive oil in a large cast iron skillet over high heat until it begins to smoke.

2. Add steaks, two at a time, and cook until both sides are brown and steak is medium rare, about 8–10 minutes total.

3. Transfer steaks to a plate covered loosely with foil while you cook the other two.

4. Serve steak with Chimichurri drizzled on top or on the side.

1 pound high-quality halibut, all skin removed, cut into bite-sized cubes

Juice from 1 orange

Juice from 1 lemon

Juice from 5 limes

⅛ cup olive oil

Salt and ground black pepper, to taste

½ red onion, thinly sliced

4 cloves of garlic, peeled and finely minced

1–2 aji amarillo chilies, thinly sliced (take out the seeds and ribs for less heat)

Handful of fresh cilantro, finely chopped

Halibut Ceviche

This is a Peruvian-style ceviche made with plenty of fresh citrus. If you can't find aji amarillo, use habaneros or serranos instead.

1. Place fish in a large, non-reactive bowl or zip-top bag.

2. Add orange, lemon and lime juices, as well as the olive oil, salt and pepper, onion, garlic, and chilies.

3. Cover the bowl or seal the bag, then refrigerate for 2–3 hours.

4. Garnish with cilantro and serve alone or with fresh tortilla chips.

INGREDIENTS | SERVES 6–8

1 (5-pound) chicken, rinsed and chopped into pieces

2 onions, roughly chopped

2 ribs celery, roughly chopped

2 carrots, roughly chopped

1 (1") piece of ginger, peeled and smashed

6–8 cloves of garlic, smashed

5 quarts water

6 medium Yukon gold potatoes, peeled and quartered

6 ounces dried egg noodles

Salt and ground black pepper, to taste

½ bunch fresh cilantro, finely chopped

4 scallions, both green and white parts, thinly sliced

2 limes, cut into wedges

2 fresh chilies (jalapeño, serrano, or Fresnos would be good), seeded and finely chopped

Peruvian Chicken Soup

This is a classic Peruvian dish that is often served for breakfast. People garnish them with their own personal mix of toppings, including hard-boiled eggs. Word is it makes a great hangover cure, too.

1. Put chicken, onions, celery, carrots, ginger, garlic, and 5 quarts cold water into a large stockpot. Bring to a boil, then reduce heat and simmer until chicken is cooked and broth is rich, about 3 hours. Skim broth as it simmers.

2. Remove chicken from broth and set aside. Strain broth to remove vegetables, then return broth to pot and place back on burner.

3. Add potatoes to broth, then bring to a boil and cook until potatoes are tender, about 20 minutes.

4. As potatoes cook, remove skin from chicken. Then pull chicken meat from bones and tear meat into shreds.

5. Turn up the heat on broth and bring to a boil. Add egg noodles and cook until just done, about 8–10 minutes.

6. Add chicken meat and let cook until heated through. Season to taste with salt and pepper.

7. Serve soup in bowls and garnish with cilantro, scallions, limes, and chilies.

Boneless Buffalo Wings

2 teaspoons salt

½ teaspoon ground pepper

¼ teaspoon cayenne pepper

1 cup flour

¼ teaspoon paprika

1 egg

1 cup milk

2 boneless skinless chicken breasts

2–4 cups cooking oil

¼ cup hot sauce of your choice

1 tablespoon margarine

These buffalo wings are a copycat of the ones served at the well-known Chili's Bar and Grill restaurants. Whip them up for your family and friends and they'll swear you ordered take-out.

1. In a medium bowl, combine salt, peppers, flour, and paprika.

2. In another bowl, whisk together the egg and milk.

3. Slice each chicken breast into bite-size pieces.

4. Preheat oil in deep fryer or skillet.

5. Dip pieces of chicken into the egg mixture 1 or 2 at a time, then into the flour/spice mixture. Repeat so that each piece of chicken is double coated.

6. When all the chicken pieces have been breaded, arrange them on a plate and chill for 15 minutes.

7. Drop each piece of chicken into hot oil and fry for 5–6 minutes, or until the breading is golden brown.

8. In a small microwave-safe bowl, combine the hot sauce and margarine. Microwave for 20–30 seconds, or just until the margarine has melted.

9. When the chicken pieces are done frying, remove them to a plate lined with paper towels to absorb the excess oil.

10. Place the chicken pieces into a covered container. Pour the sauce over the chicken, put the lid on, and shake gently until each piece of chicken is coated with sauce.

12 small jalapeños

1 (3-ounce) package low-fat cream cheese, softened

1 tablespoon lemon juice

¼ cup Super Spicy Salsa (see Chapter 7)

1 teaspoon chopped fresh oregano

Stuffed Jalapeños

These little peppers make a super appetizer. Serve them at the beginning of your next Mexican meal.

1. Cut jalapeños in half lengthwise. For a milder taste, remove membranes and seeds. Set aside.

2. In a small bowl, combine cream cheese with lemon juice; beat until fluffy. Add salsa and oregano and mix well.

3. Using a small spoon, fill each jalapeño half with the cream cheese mixture. Serve immediately or cover and chill for up to 8 hours before serving.

Working with Hot Peppers

You must use caution when working with hot peppers like jalapeños, Scotch bonnet, and habaneros. Use gloves when working with peppers and never, ever touch your face, especially your eyes, until you have removed the gloves and thoroughly washed your hands.

½ teaspoon black pepper

¼ teaspoon cayenne pepper

½ teaspoon lemon zest

½ teaspoon dried dill weed

⅛ teaspoon salt

1 tablespoon brown sugar

Olive or vegetable oil, as needed

4 (5-ounce) swordfish steaks

Cajun-Rubbed Swordfish

Any journey through the spicy foods of the United States wouldn't be complete without a nod to Cajun flavors. Plus, as an added bonus this recipe is low in both cholesterol and calories!

1. Prepare and preheat a grill. In a small bowl, combine pepper, cayenne pepper, lemon zest, dill weed, salt, and brown sugar and mix well. Sprinkle onto both sides of the swordfish steaks and rub in. Set aside for 30 minutes.

2. Brush the grill with oil. Add swordfish and cook without moving for 4 minutes. Carefully turn steaks and cook for 2–4 minutes on the second side until fish just flakes when tested with fork. Serve immediately.

CHAPTER 13

Piquillos and Paprikash: Europe

¼ cup olive oil

5 garlic cloves, peeled and roughly chopped

6 canned anchovy filets (no need to chop, they'll dissolve on their own)

1 teaspoon crushed red pepper flakes

1 (35-ounce) can of tomatoes with their juices

½ cup chopped kalamata olives

2 tablespoons capers, drained

1 pound of your favorite pasta (linguine and spaghetti are good choices here), cooked and drained

Handful fresh parsley, roughly chopped

Pasta Puttanesca

Here's a sauce that's not shy on flavor: spicy, thanks to red chili, and salty, thanks to anchovies, olives, and capers. Don't be surprised if you end up licking the bowl.

1. Heat the olive oil in a wide saucepan. Add the garlic, anchovies, and red pepper flakes, and cook until garlic is softened and anchovies begin to break up, about 4–5 minutes.

2. Add the tomatoes, stir, and break up the tomatoes with the spoon. Let simmer for 2–3 minutes.

3. Add the olives and capers, and stir. Let the sauce simmer and the flavors come together, about 5–10 minutes.

4. Put the cooked pasta in a bowl, add the sauce and toss. Sprinkle with parsley.

The Legend of Puttanesca

The culinary legend behind *puttanesca* ("whore's style sauce") is that it was devised by Italian prostitutes. The idea is that the deeply aromatic sauce would lure customers off the streets and into bordellos. This may or may not be true, but leave it to the people behind the oldest profession in the world to develop a dish that is popular to this day.

1 pound large shrimp, peeled and deveined

1 teaspoon salt

2 teaspoons crushed red pepper flakes

3 tablespoons olive oil

1 onion, thinly sliced

3 garlic cloves, peeled and finely chopped

1 (14½-ounce) can crushed tomatoes

½ cup dry white

¼ teaspoon dried oregano

Handful fresh parsley, finely chopped

Handful fresh basil leaves, finely chopped

Salt and pepper, to taste

Shrimp fra Diavolo

Fra Diavolo, *which means "brother devil" in Italian, refers to the devilishly spicy nature of the dish. Serve it with pasta or with crusty bread.*

1. Toss the shrimp in a medium bowl with the salt and red pepper flakes.

2. Heat the olive oil in a heavy skillet. Add the shrimp and sauté over medium-high heat, tossing, until shrimp are just cooked, about 2 minutes. Using a slotted spoon or fork, remove the shrimp and transfer to a plate. Set aside.

3. Add the onion and garlic to the skillet, adding a bit of oil if necessary. Sauté until they are soft and fragrant, about 3–4 minutes.

4. Add the tomatoes, wine, and oregano. Stir and simmer, uncovered, until the sauce reduces slightly, about 10–12 minutes.

5. Return the shrimp to the tomato mixture, stirring to make sure they are mixed in, and cook until shrimp are heated through and flavors mix, another 1–3 minutes.

6. Add the parsley and basil, salt and pepper to taste, and toss quickly. Transfer to serving platter.

Deveining Shrimp

The "vein" that runs down the back of a shrimp is actually its digestive track. It looks like a thin black piece of thread. Removing it, while not necessary, is easy enough to do. Once the shell has been removed, simply take a paring knife and make a shallow cut down the shrimp's back. Using the tip of the knife, start to lift out the vein. It will slip out easily.

2½ pounds ground pork (you can buy ground pork or, by all means, grind your own in a food processor or old-fashioned meat grinder)

1 teaspoon salt

½ teaspoon ground black pepper

2 teaspoons garlic, peeled and finely chopped

2 teaspoons fennel seed

1 teaspoon crushed red chili pepper flakes

1 teaspoon paprika

1 tablespoon fresh parsley, finely chopped

½ teaspoon cayenne pepper

Spicy Italian Sausage

The best sausages are typically made with lots of fat and stuffed into casings, but this simplified recipe lets you enjoy the same flavors with leaner meat and easier-to-make patties.

1. Put the pork in a large bowl. Add all the remaining ingredients and mix thoroughly. If the mixture seems too dry, add a splash of water or red wine to moisten things up.

2. If you have time, take off a small piece of meat, shape it into a ball, and cook it in a skillet over medium heat until it is brown on both sides and cooked through. Taste it and adjust seasonings if necessary.

3. Shape portions of the meat mixture into patties.

4. Heat a large skillet over medium-high heat for 2–3 minutes. (You want to get it good and hot so the sausage will sizzle and brown immediately upon hitting the skillet.)

5. Add the patties to the pan and let them cook, untouched, for about 5 minutes. When one side is brown, flip each of the patties and let the other side brown. Leave sausages in pan until they are cooked all the way through, about 12–15 minutes total.

6. Remove from pan and serve immediately.

1 pound fresh tuna, roughly chopped and pulsed in a food processor

3 tablespoons bread crumbs

1 egg, lightly beaten

Salt and pepper, to taste

½ teaspoon dried oregano

½ teaspoon ground cinnamon

½–1 teaspoon dried red pepper flakes

1 handful fresh parsley, finely chopped

2 tablespoons pine nuts

¼ cup finely grated cheese like Parmesan or Pecorino

3 cups tomato sauce, either homemade or canned

3 cups olive oil for frying

Handful of all-purpose flour, for coating meatballs

Spicy Tuna Meatballs

This Sicilian-inspired recipe uses ingredients that define the region: fresh seafood and spices that are more Spanish and Middle Eastern than classic Italian. Be sure to use fresh tuna, not canned.

1. Combine tuna, bread crumbs, egg, salt and pepper, oregano, cinnamon, chili flakes, parsley, pine nuts, and cheese in a large bowl. Using your hands, gently but thoroughly stir all the elements together so they are fully mixed.

2. Scoop the tuna mixture out by heaping tablespoons and roll between your hands to form meatballs. (Wet your hands to prevent sticking.)

3. Put the tomato sauce in a small saucepan and heat, covered, over low heat.

4. Heat the olive oil in a deep pot over medium-high heat until it reaches 350°F. (Use a thermometer to measure; the oil should stay at this temperature the whole time you are cooking the meatballs.)

5. Roll the meatballs lightly in flour and then carefully lower them into the oil. Fry until they are a light golden brown, about 2–3 minutes. With a slotted spoon, remove them to a plate covered in a paper towel to remove excess oil.

6. Serve meatballs with tomato sauce, either on their own or with pasta.

6 tablespoons olive oil

3 garlic cloves, peeled and thinly sliced lengthwise

1 fresh serrano chili (seeded, if you like), thinly sliced

Pinch of crushed red pepper flakes

1 pound spaghetti

Salt, to taste

½ bunch of fresh parsley leaves, finely chopped

Grated Parmesan cheese, for garnish

Spaghetti with Garlic and Chili Oil

This is a simple recipe, but one that you will come back to again and again. The garlic and chilies infuse the oil with a rich flavor.

1. Heat the oil in a small pan, then add the garlic, chili, and pepper flakes, and cook over low heat for 2–3 minutes, until the garlic turns golden brown. Remove the pan from the heat and set aside.

2. Cook the spaghetti in a large pot of salted water.

3. Drain the pasta and put in a large bowl. Add the garlic and chili oil and parsley, and toss.

4. Top with grated cheese and serve.

8 ounces feta cheese

1 red serrano or jalapeño chili (seeded if you like), finely chopped

2 garlic cloves, peeled and minced

4 scallions, both green and white parts, thinly sliced

½ bunch fresh parsley leaves, finely chopped

6 tablespoons olive oil

Marinated Feta Cheese

Serve this with crusty bread or crackers for a crowd-pleasing appetizer. It tastes best if you let it marinate overnight.

1. Chop feta cheese into small cubes. Place in a bowl.

2. Combine chili, garlic, scallions, parsley, and olive oil together in a bowl.

3. Pour marinade over feta cheese, cover, and put in the refrigerator. Let it marinate for at least 4 hours, overnight if possible.

4. Pull out of refrigerator and let cheese warm to room temperature before serving.

Feta Cheese

Feta is a salty, crumbly cheese that is synonymous with Greek cuisine. It's used in every imaginable way in Greece: in salads, as a table cheese, in savory pastries, and even drizzled with honey. While many types of similar cheese purport to be feta, since 2002 it's been European law that feta is "protected designation of origin product." In order to truly be called feta, a cheese must be produced in Greece and made from only sheep's or goat's milk.

2 pounds ground pork

2 teaspoons salt

3 cloves of garlic, peeled and finely chopped

2 tablespoons Spanish smoked paprika (available at specialty food stores)

1 teaspoon ground black pepper

1 teaspoon light brown sugar

1 teaspoon red chili pepper flakes

Handful fresh parsley leaves, finely chopped

Spanish Chorizo Sausage

Spanish chorizo, which differs from the chorizo made and eaten throughout Mexico, gets its distinct flavor from smoked paprika. The chorizo is often cured, and dry-aged, but this recipe gives you fresh sausage patties with the same flavors.

1. Put the pork in a large bowl. Add all the remaining ingredients and mix thoroughly. If the mixture seems too dry, add a splash of water or red wine to moisten things up.

2. If you have time, take off a small piece of meat, shape it into a ball, and cook it in a skillet over medium heat until it is brown on both sides and cooked through. Taste it and adjust seasonings if necessary.

3. Shape portions of the meat mixture into patties.

4. Heat a large skillet over medium-high heat for 2–3 minutes. (You want to get it good and hot so the sausage will sizzle and brown immediately upon hitting the skillet.)

5. Add the patties to the pan and let them cook, untouched, for about 5 minutes. When one side is brown, flip each of the patties and let the other side brown. Leave sausages in pan until they are cooked all the way through, about 12–15 minutes total.

6. Remove from pan and serve immediately.

Smoked Paprika

Spanish smoked paprika, called *pimentón,* is made by smoking red peppers, then drying and grinding them. You can find smoked paprika in a wide range of intensities from sweet and mild to bittersweet and medium-hot, as well as hot.

INGREDIENTS | SERVES 6

3 tablespoons olive oil, divided

1 large onion, chopped

2 garlic cloves, peeled and finely chopped

½ pound Spanish chorizo, crumbled

2 teaspoons smoked or hot paprika

1½ pounds potatoes, peeled, and cut into large chunks

8 cups chicken broth or water

1 pound kale, stemmed and roughly chopped

Handful fresh parsley leaves, finely chopped

Potato and Chorizo Stew

A hearty, rich stew that's easy to make. Make it a day ahead and it will taste even better the following day.

1. Heat olive oil in large pot over medium heat. Add onion and garlic and cook until translucent, about 6 minutes.

2. Add chorizo and paprika, stir, and let cook until chorizo is browned and mostly cooked, about 5 minutes.

3. Add potatoes and broth. Turn up heat and bring to boil. Then lower heat and let simmer for 20–25 minutes.

4. Add kale, stir, and let wilt, then let simmer another 15 or so minutes.

5. Ladle into bowls and sprinkle with parsley.

2 tablespoons extra-virgin olive oil

1 teaspoon salt

1 teaspoon *pimentón* (smoked paprika) or hot paprika

¼ teaspoon cayenne pepper

¼ cup honey

1 cup whole almonds, skin on

Spanish Sweet and Spicy Almonds

Almonds grow everywhere in Spain, so these are a tapas menu staple.

1. Preheat oven to 350°F.

2. Combine the olive oil, salt, paprika, cayenne pepper, and honey in a bowl with a fork. Add the almonds and stir to coat.

3. Pour the coated almonds onto a baking sheet lined with nonstick foil and separate them into individual nuts with a fork.

4. Bake for 10 minutes, stir the nuts around, and bake another 5 minutes. Let cool on the foil and then break them into individual nuts and store them in a tin with a tight-fitting lid.

Extra Almond Spice

While the almonds are still warm, sprinkle them with a mixture of equal parts sugar and salt and a big pinch of cayenne pepper and ground cinnamon. Then let them cool. They will have a frosty coating of spicy crystals when they harden.

5 ounces goat cheese, brought to room temperature

½ teaspoon red pepper flakes

1 garlic clove, finely chopped

2 (12-ounce) jars of Spanish piquillo peppers, drained

3 tablespoons olive oil

Salt and pepper, to taste

Stuffed Piquillo Peppers

Piquillo peppers are grown only in Navarre in northern Spain, where the freshly picked peppers are grilled over beechwood fires and packed in oil. They have a wonderful spicy, sweet, and smoky flavor.

1. Combine the goat cheese, pepper flakes, and garlic in a small bowl.

2. Using your fingers, carefully open each of the piquillo peppers at the stem end. Gently stuff each with about ½ teaspoon of goat cheese. Place peppers in a single layer on a baking dish. Pour the olive oil over the peppers.

3. Set the broiler to high. Broil the peppers for 8–10 minutes, or until the cheese is soft and bubbly.

4. Sprinkle with salt and pepper and serve.

⅓ cup extra-virgin olive oil, or more as needed

4 large garlic cloves, thinly sliced lengthwise

1½ pounds shrimp, peeled and deveined

Salt and pepper, to taste

1 teaspoon ground cumin

1½ teaspoons smoked or hot paprika

½ teaspoon cayenne pepper

Handful fresh parsley, finely chopped

Spicy Shrimp Tapas

This is one of the easiest recipes imaginable, but it tastes luxurious. Drink it with a glass of wine and pretend you're in a tapas bar in Spain.

1. Over low heat, warm the olive oil in a large skillet. Add the garlic and cook until it turns golden, 2–3 minutes.

2. Turn the heat to medium-high and add the shrimp, salt and pepper, cumin, paprika, and cayenne pepper. Stir to combine then cook, turning the shrimp once or twice until they are nice and pink and the oil is bubbly, about 8–10 minutes.

3. Garnish with parsley and serve.

Tapas

Tapas, which are small plates of food similar to appetizers, are practically a way of life in Spain. Tapas bars, some of which bring you complimentary plates of food as long as you keep drinking glasses of wine, are filled with people night after night. People often make a meal out of tapas by ordering an array and grazing for most of the evening.

1 pound dried red kidney beans

1 tablespoon olive oil

1 onion, diced

1 green bell pepper, cored and diced

3 cloves garlic, minced

2 hot red peppers, minced

½ pound linguica sausage, chopped

1 pound ground beef

1 (14-ounce) can diced tomatoes

1 (8-ounce) can tomato sauce

2 tablespoons chili powder

¼ teaspoon cloves

1 cup beef broth

1 teaspoon Tabasco

Salt and pepper, to taste

⅓ cup minced parsley

Portuguese Chili with Red Beans

The broth from the cooked red beans adds to the flavor and texture of this chili. You can use canned beans, but the end result will be different.

1. Rinse red beans; pick out any bits of soil or discolored beans. Place in a large bowl; fill with water to cover by several inches. Soak several hours, or overnight.

2. Drain; place in a tall soup pot and cover with fresh water. Bring to a boil over high heat; reduce heat. Simmer until beans are tender, about 3 hours. Add water as needed, but after cooking broth should be thick.

3. In a heavy Dutch oven over high heat, combine oil, onion, bell pepper, garlic, and hot red peppers; sauté 3 minutes.

4. Add sausage and beef; continue cooking until ground beef is no longer pink. Drain fat; add tomatoes, tomato sauce, chili powder, cloves, and broth. Stir in beans with cooking broth and Tabasco. Reduce heat to medium; simmer 1 hour, stirring often and adding small amounts of liquid if needed.

5. Add salt and pepper. Remove from heat; stir in parsley. Serve with crusty bread and extra hot sauce.

Linguica Sausage

Linguica is a mild Portuguese sausage that is smoked. It is flavored with spices like oregano, paprika, cumin, and cinnamon. It's served in many forms, such as plain alongside bread, in rice, or inside soups and stews. Look for linguica in specialty food stores.

2½ pounds chicken legs and thighs

Salt and pepper, to taste

½ cup flour, for dredging

4 tablespoons vegetable oil

2 tablespoons hot paprika

½ teaspoon cayenne pepper

1 red bell pepper, stemmed, seeded, and cored, sliced into strips

2 tomatoes, seeded, roughly chopped

1 large onion, roughly chopped

1½ cups chicken stock or water

¾ cup sour cream

Handful fresh parsley leaves, finely chopped

Chicken Paprikash

A classic Hungarian dish, this is one of the most simple, comforting winter meals imaginable. Serve it with noodles, dumplings, or potatoes.

1. Season the chicken pieces with salt and pepper. Put the flour on a plate and dredge the chicken in it, shaking off excess flour.

2. Over medium-high heat, heat oil in large Dutch oven. Cook chicken, skin side down first, turning once, until brown, about 10 minutes. Remove from pan and set aside.

3. Add paprika, peppers, tomatoes, and onions to pot, adding a little more oil if necessary. Cook, over medium heat, until onions are soft, about 5 minutes.

4. Return chicken to pot. Add broth and bring to boil. Reduce heat and let simmer, covered, until chicken is fully cooked, about 15 minutes.

5. In a small bowl, whisk together sour cream and ¾ cup sauce from the pot. (You need to temper the sour cream before adding it so it doesn't curdle in the pot.) Stir sour cream mixture into the pot. Mix well and let ingredients cook together on low heat another 2 minutes.

6. Garnish with parsley and serve.

3 tablespoons vegetable oil

1 large onion, chopped

3 garlic cloves, finely minced

2 tablespoons hot paprika

½ teaspoon ground caraway

1 teaspoon cayenne pepper

2 pounds pork stew meat, such as pork shoulder, cut into 1" pieces

1 quart chicken stock or water

2 tomatoes, roughly chopped

1 red pepper, seeded and roughly chopped

2 potatoes, cubed

Spicy Pork Goulash

A traditional Hungarian dish, goulash is more of a soup than a stew. You can serve it over rice for a heartier meal.

1. Over low-medium heat, heat the oil in a large Dutch oven. Add the onion, garlic, paprika, caraway, and cayenne until onion is softened, about 6–8 minutes.

2. Turn up the heat and add the pork, give it a good stir, and cook until pork is browned, 8 minutes.

3. Add the stock or water and bring to a boil. Lower the heat and let simmer, covered, for 40–60 minutes, until pork is tender.

4. Add tomatoes and bell pepper; let simmer for another 15 minutes.

5. Add the potatoes and let simmer until potatoes are cooked, about 20 minutes.

6. Ladle into bowls and serve.

3 tablespoons butter

2 onions, chopped

½ teaspoon hot paprika

Pinch red pepper flakes

1½ pounds cabbage, shredded or very thinly sliced

½ cup chicken stock or water

1 apple, peeled, cored, and thinly sliced

1 cup light cream

Pinch of paprika

Pinch of salt

Cabbage with Paprika

Apples give this earthy, spicy dish a bit of sweetness, while the cream gives it a cooling effect.

1. Melt the butter in a skillet. Add the onions and cook at a low-medium heat until they are softened, about 5 minutes.

2. Add the paprika, chili flakes, and cabbage, and stir. Cook over high heat for 2–3 minutes. Lower the heat, add the stock, cover and let simmer for 20–25 minutes until cabbage is soft.

3. Add the apple to the pan, mix well, and cook until apple is heated through, another 3–4 minutes. Remove pan from heat.

4. Combine cream, paprika, and salt in a small bowl.

5. Transfer cabbage to serving dish and pour cream over cabbage. Serve.

CHAPTER 14

The Spicy Route:
Africa and The Middle East

¾ cup olive oil

1 tablespoon hot paprika

2 teaspoons ground cumin

2 cloves of garlic, finely minced

Salt and pepper, to taste

2 pounds beef sirloin or tenderloin, cut into 1" cubes

1 green bell pepper, stemmed, seeded, cut into 1" squares

1 red bell pepper, stemmed, seeded, cut into 1" squares

1 onion, cut

4 firm tomatoes, seeded and cut into eighths

4 large jalapeño chilies, seeded, cut into ¾" lengths

Beef Shish Kebabs

Serve these beef kebabs straight on the skewer or slide them off and serve alongside rice. If you don't have access to a grill, cook them under the broiler.

1. In large bowl, the olive oil, spices, garlic, and salt and pepper. Add the meat and combine. Make sure all the pieces are coated with marinade. Cover with plastic wrap, put in the refrigerator and let marinate for at least 2 hours, overnight if possible.

2. Thread the meat, bell peppers, tomatoes, onions, and jalapeños on skewers.

3. Cook the kebabs on a grill or in the oven under a low broiler. Cook for about 7 minutes per side, or until desired doneness.

Skewers

You can use either metal or bamboo skewers to cook the kebabs. If using metal, be sure to be careful when removing them from the grill as they will be hot. If using bamboo, remember to soak the skewers in water for 15 minutes beforehand so they do not catch fire.

1 cup cracked bulgur wheat (available at most supermarkets or specialty food stores)

1 pound ground beef or lamb

1 large onion, finely chopped

1 tablespoon ground cumin

2 teaspoons ground cayenne pepper

Salt, to taste

3 cups oil for deep-frying

For the Filling:

1 onion, finely chopped

2 tablespoons olive oil

½ pound ground beef or lamb

1 tablespoon sumac (optional)

1 teaspoon ground cinnamon

½ cup pine nuts

Salt, to taste

Kibbeh

Kibbeh, Lebanese meatballs typically have an outer shell of bulgur wheat stuffed with ground meat and spices. For a shortcut version, combine all the ingredients (for the outer dough and the filling), roll into balls, then fry.

1. Place the bulgur wheat in a bowl and cover with cold water. Let it sit for 15 minutes so the wheat can absorb the water and soften. Drain.

2. In a separate bowl combine the meat, onion, and spices. Add the bulgur and mix well. Cover and place in the refrigerator for 1 hour.

3. Meanwhile, make the filling. Fry the onions in the olive oil until they are translucent. Add the ground meat and fry over medium heat until the meat is browned. Add the spices and pine nuts and cook another few minutes. Take off heat and set aside.

4. Take the bulgur mixture out of the refrigerator. To make the kibbeh, take an egg-sized amount of bulgur mixture and roll it into a ball. Poke a hole in the ball with your finger to make space for the filling. Stuff with 2 teaspoons of filling and then pinch the ball closed, sealing the kibbeh.

5. Heat the frying oil in a saucepan. Deep-fry the kibbeh for about 4 minutes, until they are golden brown.

6. Remove kibbeh from frying oil with a slotted spoon and place on a plate lined with a paper towel to absorb excess oil. Serve immediately.

2 large onions, thinly sliced

1 cup brown lentils, picked through for stones

Salt and pepper, to taste

1 cup long-grain white rice

1½ cups water

1 cup elbow macaroni

2 tablespoons olive oil

2 garlic cloves, peeled and finely chopped

½ teaspoon cumin

½ teaspoon coriander

½ teaspoon crushed red pepper flakes

2½ cups tomato sauce (homemade or from a can)

2 tablespoons white or red wine vinegar

Koshary

Koshary is one of Egypt's national dishes. Koshary is perfect match for Harissa (see Chapter 6).

1. Begin caramelizing your onions. They will take a bit of time, so start them first and keep an eye on them.

2. Put the lentils in a pot and cover with water, seasoning with salt and pepper. Bring lentils to a boil, then turn heat to medium and let boil until tender, about 30 minutes. Drain.

3. Combine rice with 1½ cups water in a pot. Cover, bring to a boil, turn heat to low, then let simmer till done, about 15 minutes.

4. Cook macaroni in boiling water until done. Drain.

5. Heat olive oil in the bottom of a saucepan, add garlic and spices, sauté until garlic is soft and fragrant. Add tomato sauce and vinegar, let simmer on stove for 10 minutes or so.

6. Check on caramelized onions. When they are done, remove from heat and set aside.

7. Assemble koshary, starting with a scoop of rice, then a scoop of lentils. Add a layer of macaroni, then cover with tomato sauce. Top with caramelized onions. Serve with a dollop of Harissa hot sauce.

Caramelizing Onions

Heat some oil on high heat in a heavy-bottomed pan, add thinly sliced onions, stir to coat evenly. Turn the heat to low and let the onions cook slowly, stirring occasionally. As they start to darken, stir frequently so they do not burn. Cook until they are deep, dark brown. It should take about 30 minutes.

Ethiopian Lamb Stew

INGREDIENTS | SERVES 6

4 tablespoons unsalted butter

1 medium red onion, thinly sliced

1½ pounds lamb stew meat, cut into ½"cubes

1½ tablespoons Berbere (see Chapter 10)

½ teaspoon ground cardamom

½ teaspoon ground ginger

¼ teaspoon ground cumin

4 garlic cloves, peeled and roughly chopped

1½ cups canned tomatoes, roughly chopped

2 jalapeño chilies, seeded and thinly sliced

½ cup dry red wine

This wonderful stew relies on the complex spice mix called berbere *that is a staple of Ethiopian cooking. For all its rich flavors, it takes a surprisingly short amount of time to make. Typically it is served with a flat, sour bread called* injera, *but it is also delicious with rice or noodles.*

1. Melt the butter in a large, heavy-bottomed skillet over high heat. Add the onions and cook, stirring constantly, until they begin to brown.

2. Add the lamb and stir-fry until the meat is browned on all sides.

3. Add the Berbere, other spices, and garlic, being careful to turn your head to avoid the spicy fumes that will rise when you add them. Stir so that the meat is evenly coated with spices.

4. Add the tomatoes, jalapeños, and wine. Stir, then turn heat to low and let simmer for another 10–15 minutes until lamb is tender and sauce has thickened.

Injera Bread

Ethiopian meals are all served, sans utensils, on top of large rounds of a flatbread called *injera*. *Injera* is made from teff flour, a grain cultivated throughout the country. It is slightly sour with a unique, spongy texture that makes it perfect for sopping up sauces. You might be able to purchase *injera* at an African or Ethiopian market.

2 cups red lentils

½ cup olive oil

1 red onion, finely chopped

2 garlic cloves, peeled and minced

1 tablespoon finely chopped jalapeño peppers

4 tomatoes, roughly chopped

Juice of 1 lemon

3 teaspoons Berbere (see Chapter 10)

1 tablespoon fresh parsley, minced

Salt, to taste

Ethiopian Lentil Stew

The Ethiopian spice mix Berbere can make anything taste extraordinary, even a humble stew of lentils. Sprinkle some raw, chopped jalapeños on top for extra heat.

1. Put lentils in large pot and cover by at least 2" with salted water. Bring to a boil, then reduce heat and let simmer until tender, about 15–20 minutes. Drain well and set aside.

2. Heat olive oil in a large skillet or sauté pan. Add the onion, garlic, and jalapeños and sauté until the onion is soft and translucent, about 5 minutes.

3. Add the lentils, tomatoes, lemon juice, Berbere, parsley, and salt. Stir to combine.

4. Cook mixture on low heat until everything is heated through, about 3–4 minutes.

4 bone-in chicken thighs (you can take the skin off or leave it on)

¾ cup Piri Piri Sauce (see Chapter 6)

2 tablespoons olive oil

Lime wedges

Piri Piri Chicken

Piri Piri, the national dish of Mozambique, is sweet, tart, spicy, and totally addictive. You can also use the sauce as a marinade for seafood; it works particularly well with shrimp.

1. Toss the chicken thighs with the Piri Piri Sauce in a large bowl. Cover and refrigerate for 20–30 minutes.

2. Heat the olive oil in a large skillet. Add the chicken (if you've left the skin on, cook the skin side down first) and cook, flipping once, about 5–7 minutes per side.

3. Make sure the chicken is fully cooked throughout before serving.

2 tablespoons olive oil

2 garlic cloves, peeled and finely chopped

1 small onion, finely chopped

1 large tomato, seeded and roughly chopped, separated into two equal portions

½ teaspoon chili powder

½ teaspoon ground cumin

1 (19-ounce) can of fava beans, with liquid

1 small cucumber, peeled, seeded, and finely chopped

2 jalapeño peppers, seeded and finely chopped

Handful of fresh parsley and mint leaves, finely chopped

Juice of half a lemon

½ cup olive oil

Foul

Foul (pronounced "FOOL") is a classic Egyptian breakfast. A far cry from sugary sweet cereal, it's spicy and satisfying and tastes best when scooped with pieces of warm pita or crusty French bread.

1. Heat olive oil in the bottom of a sauce pan. Add garlic, onion, half the tomatoes, chili powder, and cumin. Sauté until soft and fragrant, about 3–4 minutes.

2. Add the fava beans and liquid. Bring to a boil, then lower heat and let simmer for 10–15 minutes. Remove from heat and let cool. Drain beans and reserve the liquid.

3. Put beans in a large bowl and toss with cucumber, jalapeño peppers, herbs, lemon juice, and olive oil. If you like a little more sauce, add a little of the reserved cooking liquid.

4. Serve in bowls with pita or French bread.

Fava Beans

Fava beans are native to north Africa and used throughout northern African and Middle Eastern cooking. Fava beans are a key ingredient in staple dishes like falafel, soups, and stews. If you can't find fava beans at the store, you can substitute canned or dried brown beans.

1½ pounds okra, cut into 1" pieces

2 tablespoons vegetable oil

2 medium onions, thinly sliced

½ teaspoon fresh ginger, finely minced

2 tomatoes, seeded and roughly chopped

2 Thai bird's eye chilies, seeded, finely chopped

2 garlic cloves, peeled and finely minced

Salt and pepper, to taste

Spicy Okra and Tomatoes

Generally, people either love okra or hate it—there's almost no in between. Native to Africa and used in Southern American cooking, okra pods add unique color and texture to the dinner table. Look for pods that are uniform in color, without any dark or soft spots.

1. Bring a saucepan of salted water to a boil. Add the okra, lower the heat, and let simmer for about 3–4 minutes. Drain okra and set aside.

2. Over high heat, heat the oil in a large frying pan. Add the onions, ginger, tomatoes, and chilies, and sauté until the onions are soft and fragrant, about 5 minutes.

3. Lower the heat to medium, add the garlic, and sauté until garlic is soft, another 3–4 minutes.

4. Add the okra, salt and pepper to taste, and cook until okra is just heated through, about 2–3 minutes.

What Makes Okra Slimy?

One of the reasons people are turned off by okra is because it has a natural slime. (There's no polite way to put it.) Okra is part of the mallow family, a group of plants that exude a gelatinous substance when cut. The slime is perfectly edible and, some might say, pleasant. Give it a try, you might even come to like it.

1½ pounds small zucchinis

½ cup Chermoula (see Chapter 6)

Zucchini with Chermoula

This dish packs a wonderful amount of flavor and, even better, takes very little effort to make. Instead of baking, feel free to pan-fry or grill the zucchini.

1. Wash the zucchini, cut off the ends, then slice them, lengthwise into ¼" thick pieces.

2. Rub the zucchini slices with the Chermoula and let marinate for 15–20 minutes.

3. Heat the oven to 350°F. Place the zucchini on a cookie sheet or baking dish. Bake 30–40 minutes, until zucchini is cooked but still a bit firm.

4. Serve zucchini hot or cold.

INGREDIENTS | SERVES 2

1 pound meaty white fish such as halibut or flounder

Salt, to taste

½ cup Chermoula (see Chapter 6)

Half a lemon, cut into thin slices

Chermoula Roasted Fish

Once you've made the Chermoula sauce, it's the easiest way to make super flavorful dishes without a lot of fuss. In its home territory of Morocco, Chermoula is a classic marinade for fish.

1. Heat the oven to 450°F.

2. As the oven comes to temperature, sprinkle fish with a little salt and spoon the Chermoula over the fish and gently massage the marinade into the flesh. Let sit.

3. When the oven is hot, place the fish, skin side down, into a roasting pan. Place lemon slices on top of fish. Roast the fish until done, about 10 minutes per inch of thickness.

2 tablespoons butter

1 large onion, finely chopped

2 carrots, finely chopped

2 cups red lentils, picked through for stones

½ teaspoon hot paprika

½ teaspoon red pepper flakes

½ teaspoon cumin

4 cups meat or vegetable stock

2 tablespoons lemon juice

Salt and pepper, to taste

Handful of chopped cilantro or parsley, for garnish

Curried Red Lentil Soup

This simple, hearty soup can be made as spicy as you like. For a different dimension of spice, chop up fresh jalapeños or serranos and use them as a garnish.

1. Melt the butter in the bottom of a pot. Add the onion and carrots and sauté until they are softened, about 3–4 minutes.

2. Add the lentils and spices and stir, making sure all the lentils are coated.

3. Add the stock. Bring to a boil, then lower the heat and let simmer for 20 minutes or until the lentils are soft. Add the lemon juice and stir. Taste and season with salt and pepper.

4. If you like, you can purée the soup in a blender or with a handheld blender. If you like a chunkier soup, skip blending.

5. Serve in bowls, garnished with fresh herbs.

What Are Lentils?

Lentils, like beans and peas, are legumes, types of flowering plants that have been cultivated since ancient Egypt. Lentils themselves are the edible seeds of the plant and they come in a wide variety of colors and sizes. Red lentils, which cook down to a more yellow color, are among the most common, along with brown and yellow. There are also small, deep green French *de Puy* lentils, which have earned the nickname "poor man's caviar."

½ cup Harissa (see Chapter 6)

½ cup plain yogurt

1 tablespoon fresh lemon juice

4 whole chicken legs (about 2 pounds; you can substitute chicken thighs or breasts if you prefer)

Harissa Roasted Chicken

Combining Harissa with yogurt not only gives chicken great flavor, the yogurt also helps tenderize the meat and keep it moist. You can use whatever cut of chicken you prefer.

1. In a small bowl, combine the Harissa, yogurt, and lemon juice. In a re-sealable plastic bag, combine marinade with chicken legs. Let stand at room temperature for 30 minutes to 1 hour.

2. Heat the oven to 425°F. When oven is hot, pull out the chicken legs and place in roasting pan. Roast the chicken for 45 minutes, or until meat is cooked through and the skin is crisp and browned.

2 pounds ground lamb

½ pound ground beef

1 teaspoon ground cumin

1 teaspoon ground coriander

1 teaspoon cayenne pepper

3 garlic cloves, peeled and finely chopped

2 teaspoons Harissa (see Chapter 6)

2 teaspoons salt

2 tablespoons fresh parsley, finely chopped

Merguez Sausage

Merguez is a spicy North African sausage made from lamb or beef. Although sausage is typically made with pork, many people in North Africa follow Islamic law and abstain from pork. Sausage is usually stuffed into casings, but this recipe skips that step to simplify things.

1. Combine the ground lamb, ground beef, spices, garlic, Harissa, salt, and parsley in a large bowl. Mix well until everything is combined. (This is easier to do with your hands.)

2. Cover the meat mixture and refrigerate for at least one hour so that the flavors can come together.

3. Shape the sausage into golf ball–sized balls using wet hands to prevent sticking. Place the meatballs in a baking dish.

4. Set the oven to broil. Position the oven rack so it is about 4" from the heat source. Broil the meatballs until they are fully cooked inside, around 8 minutes. Check them once to flip them or shake the pan to make sure they cook evenly.

4 tablespoons olive oil

4 red bell peppers, stemmed and seeded, cut into ½" pieces

5 garlic cloves, finely chopped

1½ pounds tomatoes, roughly chopped

1 teaspoon hot paprika

Salt and pepper, to taste

½ teaspoon red wine vinegar

Tunisian Fried Pepper Salad

This salad, which is also known as marmouma *or* chouka, *makes an unexpected but delightful side dish or appetizer. Feel free to turn up the heat with more hot pepper. Serve it with crusty bread and, if you like, goat cheese.*

1. Heat the olive oil in a frying pan. Add the pepper slices and fry over low heat, turning them every so often until they are soft.

2. Add the garlic and cook until the garlic is softened and the peppers are lightly browned.

3. Add the tomatoes, paprika, salt, and pepper. Give the whole mixture a gentle stir and then simmer, uncovered, until the tomatoes are reduced to a very thick consistency, about 20–25 minutes.

4. Taste the mixture. If it tastes too sweet, add the red wine vinegar.

5. Serve on top or alongside slices of crusty bread.

1 (15-ounce) can of chickpeas, drained, liquid reserved

Juice of 2 lemons

3 garlic cloves, peeled and roughly chopped

4 tablespoons tahini (ground sesame paste)

3 tablespoons olive oil

1 teaspoon hot paprika

¼ teaspoon red chili pepper flakes

Salt and pepper, to taste

Spicy Hummus

Hummus has become a very popular dip around the world. Here, it gets an unexpected twist with some hot peppers. You might also try stirring in some Zhug (see Chapter 6) for even more heat. Serve with pita bread or alongside grilled meats and rice.

1. Put the chickpeas, along with a few teaspoons of their liquid, into a food processor or blender. Blend to a rough paste.

2. Add the lemon juice, garlic, tahini, olive oil, paprika, and chili flakes. Blend until it makes a very smooth paste, adding chickpea liquid as necessary. Season with salt and pepper.

Tahini

Tahini is a paste made from ground sesame seeds. It's a common ingredient in North African and Middle Eastern cuisine, where it is made from hulled and lightly roasted sesame seeds. You should be able to find tahini at most large supermarkets or specialty stores. Be sure to give it a good stir before using, as the paste will settle on the bottom and all the oil will rise to the top.

CHAPTER 15

Curries, Stir-Fry, and More: Asia

2 tablespoons vegetable oil

½ onion, chopped

4 tablespoons Green Curry Paste (see Chapter 6)

1 (15-ounce) can coconut milk

1 package firm tofu, drained and cut into cubes

2 carrots, sliced

1 red bell pepper, seeded and cut into chunks

1 cup snow peas

Handful fresh basil leaves, roughly chopped

Handful fresh cilantro leaves, roughly chopped

Thai Green Curry Tofu

Use this recipe as a guideline, adding or using different vegetables according to your own preference, and using as much or as little Green Curry Paste as like. Serve with white or brown rice.

1. Heat oil in a wok or large, deep-frying pan over medium-high heat. Add onions and sauté 1–2 minutes. Add Green Curry Paste and stir-fry until fragrant, about 2–3 minutes.

2. Add the coconut milk and stir until both ingredients come together. Add the tofu and stir to combine. Cover and let simmer for 5 minutes.

3. Add carrots, bell pepper, and snow peas. Stir and cook 3–5 minutes, until vegetables are cooked through but still firm and crisp.

4. Transfer to serving bowl and sprinkle with fresh basil and cilantro.

2 tablespoons vegetable oil

½ onion, chopped

2 cloves of garlic, peeled and finely chopped

4 tablespoons Red Curry Paste (see Chapter 6)

1½ pounds chicken meat, thinly sliced

1 (15-ounce) can of coconut milk

2 Chinese or Japanese eggplants, cut into cubes

1 cup of green beans, sliced into 1"-long pieces

Handful fresh basil leaves, finely chopped

Thai Red Curry Chicken

Use chicken breast, thighs, or legs—whatever you prefer. And use more curry paste if you want more heat.

1. Heat oil in a wok or large, deep skillet over medium-high heat. Add onion and garlic and sauté for 1–2 minutes. Add curry paste and stir-fry until fragrant, about 2–3 minutes.

2. Turn heat up slightly, add chicken and stir-fry until chicken is browned on all sides and mostly cooked, about 5 minutes.

3. Add coconut milk and stir well to combine all ingredients. Bring to a boil, then turn heat down and let simmer until chicken is cooked, 8–10 minutes.

4. Add eggplant and green beans and let cook until vegetables are cooked through but not soggy, 6–8 minutes.

5. Taste curry and adjust seasoning if necessary.

6. Transfer to serving bowl and sprinkle with fresh basil.

Eggplants

Eggplants come in different shapes and sizes, not just the large, Grimace-shaped ones you see in most grocery stores. Chinese eggplants (also sometimes called Japanese eggplants, depending on where you shop) are longer and more narrow than typical eggplants. The flavor does not differ much, so if you can't find these slender eggplants, just use the eggplant that is readily available.

1 tablespoon lime juice

1 tablespoon fish sauce

1 tablespoon dark, sweet soy sauce

3 tablespoons chopped onion

1 teaspoon honey

1 teaspoon dried chili powder

1 green onion, trimmed and thinly sliced

1 teaspoon chopped cilantro

1½ pound sirloin steak

Salt and pepper, to taste

Hot and Sour Beef

This is a good dish to serve as an introduction to Thai flavors. Diners can add as little or as much of the sauce as they prefer.

1. Make the sauce by thoroughly combining the first 8 ingredients; set aside.

2. Season the steak with salt and pepper, then grill or broil it to your preferred doneness. Remove the steak from the grill, cover with foil, and let rest for 5–10 minutes.

3. Thinly slice the steak, cutting across the grain.

4. Arrange the pieces on a serving platter. Spoon the sauce over the top. Serve with rice.

Sirloin Steak

Sirloin steak is a steak cut that comes from the back portion of the cow. It continues off the back end of the short loin, which is where T-bone and porterhouse steaks are cut. Sirloin is divided into top and bottom, with the top section being more tender. The best sirloin meat will be labeled "top sirloin."

½ cup rice vinegar

½ cup fish sauce

¼ cup sesame oil

¼ cup chili oil

¼ cup lime juice

2 cups long-grain rice (preferably Jasmine)

4–6 green onions, trimmed and thinly sliced

2 carrots, peeled and diced

1 sweet red pepper, seeded and diced

1 serrano chili pepper, seeded and minced

¼–½ cup chopped mint

¼–½ cup chopped cilantro

1 pound cooked shrimp

⅓ cup chopped unsalted peanuts

Spicy Rice Salad

This salad also works well with shredded chicken instead of the shrimp. If you would prefer a vegetarian salad, simply omit any meat.

1. Make the dressing by whisking together rice vinegar, fish sauce, sesame oil, chili oil, and lime juice. Set aside.

2. Cook the rice. Fluff the rice with a fork, then transfer it to a large mixing bowl. Allow the rice to cool slightly.

3. Pour approximately ⅓ of the dressing over the rice and fluff to coat. Continue to fluff the rice every so often until it is completely cooled.

4. Add the green onions, carrots, red pepper, serrano chili pepper, mint, cilantro, and shrimp to the rice. Toss with the remaining dressing.

5. To serve, place on individual plates and garnish with peanuts.

1 tablespoon vegetable oil

1 pound (medium-sized) raw shrimp, peeled and deveined, shells reserved

2 quarts fish or chicken stock

1 quart water

3 stalks lemongrass, peeled and chopped

Zest of 1 lime, grated

6–8 kaffir lime leaves

10 (⅛"-thick) slices fresh ginger

2 fresh serrano chilies, seeded and chopped

24 fresh mussels, cleaned

2 tablespoons lime juice

2 tablespoons fish sauce

3 tablespoons chopped fresh cilantro

Red pepper flakes, to taste

¼ cup sliced green onions

Salt, to taste

Spicy Thai Seafood Soup

Many cultures have their own spicy seafood soup. You can think of this Thai soup and French bouillabaisse as different sides of the same coin.

1. Heat the vegetable oil in a large saucepan. Add the shrimp shells and sauté until they turn bright pink. Add the stock, water, lemongrass, lime zest, lime leaves, ginger, and serrano chilies. Bring to a boil, reduce heat, and simmer for 30 minutes. Strain the broth into a clean soup pot.

2. Bring the broth to a boil. Add the mussels, cover, and cook until the shells open, about 2 minutes. Use a slotted spoon to remove the mussels, discarding any that have not opened. Remove the top shell of each mussel and discard. Set aside the mussels on the half shell.

3. Add the shrimp to the boiling broth and cook until they are opaque, about 2 minutes. Reduce heat to low.

4. Add the mussels to the pot. Stir in the lime juice, fish sauce, cilantro, red pepper flakes, and green onions. Simmer for 1–2 minutes. Season to taste with salt.

5. Serve immediately.

INGREDIENTS | SERVES 4–6

2 tablespoons vegetable oil

3 tablespoons Red Curry Paste (see Chapter 6)

6 cups chicken or vegetable broth

1 pound green beans, trimmed

Curried Green Beans

Green beans taste great just barely cooked and with plenty of snap. But in this instance, you have to cook the beans until they are soft. As the beans break down, they help form the sauce.

1. In a large saucepan, heat the vegetable oil over medium-high heat.

2. Add the curry paste and stir-fry for 1 minute.

3. Stir in the broth until well combined with the paste. Add the green beans and bring to a low boil. Cook for 15–20 minutes to reduce the liquid.

4. Reduce the heat to maintain a hard simmer and continue cooking until the beans are very well done.

5. Serve the beans over steamed rice, ladling the sauce over the top.

2 tablespoons peanut oil

1 tablespoon sesame oil

½ pound ground pork

2 garlic cloves, peeled and minced

1 tablespoon fresh ginger, minced

2 leeks, white parts only, thinly sliced

1 tablespoon fermented Chinese black beans (optional)

2 teaspoons ground Szechuan peppercorns

1 teaspoon crushed red pepper flakes

1 cup chicken stock

2 teaspoons soy sauce

2 tablespoons cornstarch mixed with 3 tablespoons cold water

1 package silken tofu, drained and cut into ½" cubes

4 scallions, thinly sliced (optional)

Handful fresh cilantro leaves, thinly sliced (optional)

Ma Po Tofu

A classic, spicy Szechuan dish from China that uses the distinct, mouth-numbing (in a good way!) Szechuan peppercorns. Adjust the amount of chili in this dish to suit your own tastes.

1. Heat the peanut and sesame oils in a wok or large frying pan over high heat. Add the pork and stir-fry until it is no longer pink.

2. Add the garlic, ginger, and leeks, and stir. Turn the heat down to medium and let cook until they are fragrant and soft, about 4–5 minutes.

3. Add the black beans, Szechuan peppercorns, and red pepper flakes. Stir well and cook for another 1–2 minutes.

4. Add the chicken stock, soy sauce, and cornstarch mixture to form the sauce. Stir well and let simmer 1–2 minutes.

5. Carefully add the tofu and gently stir so that tofu stays intact and gets coated with sauce.

6. Continue cooking on low heat until tofu is warmed through, 4–5 minutes. Serve with rice. Garnish with scallion and cilantro if desired.

Szechuan Peppercorns

Szechuan peppercorns are an ingredient you will probably never forget. A staple in Szechuan cuisine, this spice hits your lips and tongue with a tingly, numbing effect. (It's not entirely unpleasant, though it's best to be prepared for the effect.) Szechuan peppercorns are not in fact peppercorns, but actually the outer pod of a tiny fruit that grows in China. Look for them in Asian groceries.

12 dried chiles de arbol, stemmed

2 tablespoons scallions, both green and white parts, thinly sliced

2 tablespoons sesame oil

2 tablespoons rice vinegar

2 tablespoons soy sauce

12 large shiitake mushrooms, stemmed and thinly sliced

Shiitake Mushroom Salad with Chilies

A simple, spicy salad with plenty of heat and earthy mushroom flavor.

1. Grind chilies in a spice grinder or food processor until they make a fine powder. Transfer to bowl and add scallions, oil, vinegar, and soy sauce. Set dressing aside.

2. Bring a pot of salted water to boil over high heat. Add mushrooms and cook until lightly chewy, about 4–5 minutes.

3. Drain mushrooms well. Transfer them to a kitchen towel or paper towels and squeeze out as much liquid as possible.

4. Put mushrooms in a bowl and pour dressing over top. Toss and let stand for 10 minutes before serving.

Shiitake Mushrooms

Of the many varieties of mushrooms around the world, shiitakes are most strongly associated with Asian cuisine. They're used throughout Japanese, Chinese, and Korean cooking. Pronounced "she-TAH-kay," the name is derived from the Japanese word for tree. They have a very strong, earthy flavor. You can find them fresh at most grocery stores, and also dried at many Asian markets.

2–3 pounds chicken legs or thighs

½ cup soy sauce

1½ cups vinegar

4 Thai bird's eye chilies

3 bay leaves

10 garlic cloves, peeled and roughly chopped

1½ teaspoons black peppercorns

Spicy Chicken Adobo

Adobo—meat braised until tender in vinegar and soy sauce with lots of garlic—is the national dish of the Philippines. It's a cinch to make and very flavorful. You could make this dish with pork or beef as well.

1. Combine all the ingredients in a large Dutch oven or pot.

2. Bring ingredients to boil over high heat. Reduce the heat to a simmer and cook, stirring occasionally, until the chicken is thoroughly cooked and tender, about 40 minutes.

3. Remove chicken from pot and place in a baking dish. Turn the oven to broil.

4. Turn burner to medium-high heat and reduce braising liquid so that it thickens, about 15 minutes. Remove bay leaves.

5. Broil chicken until it begins to caramelize, about 5 minutes. Return chicken to pot and let cook in thickened sauce for another 3–4 minutes.

6. Serve adobo with rice and a generous drizzle of sauce.

1 carrot, peeled and cut into matchsticks

⅓ large daikon radish, peeled and cut into matchsticks

1 teaspoon salt mixed with 2 teaspoons sugar

⅓ cup sugar

1 cup white vinegar

½ cup warm water

4 crusty French rolls (or 1–2 baguettes sliced into 4 sandwich-length segments)

Mayonnaise, to taste

Soy sauce or Maggi seasoning

1 cup roasted chicken, torn into shreds

1 small cucumber, peeled and seeded and cut into spears

5 cilantro sprigs, roughly chopped

1 jalapeño pepper, thinly sliced (remove seeds and ribs for less heat)

Banh Mi Sandwiches

Banh mi are an example of the legacy left by the French on Vietnamese cuisine: crusty French rolls stuffed with pickled Asian vegetables. This is a great way to use up leftover roasted chicken, but you could use any filling you like such as pork, shrimp, tofu, or even fried eggs.

1. Make quick pickled carrot and daikon radish. Toss carrot and radish with salt-sugar mixture. Let sit for 10 minutes, until they are softened. Rinse vegetables off under cold water. Pat dry and place vegetables in non-reactive bowl.

2. Combine sugar, vinegar, and water. Pour brine over vegetables and put in refrigerator for 1 hour.

3. Take French rolls and slather insides with mayonnaise. Add a few drops of soy sauce or Maggi.

4. Stuff each sandwich with all of the fillings: chicken, cucumber spears, cilantro, and jalapeño. Remove pickled carrot and daikon from refrigerator, shake off excess brine, then add to sandwiches.

1 bunch scallions, both green and white parts, roughly chopped

10 garlic cloves, peeled and roughly chopped

¾ cup soy sauce

1 tablespoon honey

1 tablespoon sesame oil

½ teaspoon black pepper

1 teaspoon red pepper flakes

3 pounds beef short ribs, skirt steak, or sirloin, thinly sliced

1 head Boston, butter, or green leaf lettuce, separated into leaves

Gochujang (Korean chili bean paste), for serving

Beef Bulgogi

This traditional Korean barbecue is delicious and garlicky. Be sure not to overcook the meat so it will stay moist and tasty.

1. Put scallions, garlic, soy sauce, honey, sesame oil, pepper, and chili flakes in a blender. Purée until smooth, adding a little water if necessary.

2. In a large bowl or zip-top bag, combine mixture with meat. Stir well, then put in the refrigerator to marinate. You can marinate meat for 1 hour or overnight, whatever you have time for.

3. Heat a grill to very high heat, or use a grill pan on the stove. Let the grill pan get very hot, to the point of smoking.

4. Grill meat until it's cooked just beyond rare—browned on the outside but still pink on the inside.

5. Serve meat with lettuce leaves, gochujang and, if you like, white rice. Wrap meat inside leaves with rice and dip into gochujang.

Gochujang

Gochujang is a pungent, fermented hot pepper paste that is used throughout Korean cuisine. It's made from ground, dried chili peppers combined with glutinous rice powder and soybean paste. It's left to naturally ferment over years in large earthenware pots. You can find gochujang at Asian groceries and Korean markets. Gochujang has a very strong flavor; a little goes a long way.

2 tablespoons vegetable oil

4 cups kimchi, cut into bite-sized pieces

1 tablespoon gochujang

4–5 cups cold rice

1 tablespoon sesame oil

Salt and pepper, to taste

4 fried eggs

Handful scallions, finely chopped, for garnish

Kimchi Fried Rice

This is great way to use up old rice. It's also a good introduction to using kimchi, whose strong flavor might take a bit of getting used to. Make sure your fried eggs have a runny yolk, which will help form a sauce of sorts.

1. Over medium-high heat, heat oil in a large skillet. Add kimchi and fry until it is heated through, about 4 minutes.

2. Add gochujang and stir to combine.

3. Add rice. Use a wooden spoon or spatula to break up the rice and stir well to ensure it is well coated and mixed with kimchi and pepper paste. You might want to add just a little bit of water to help loosen the rice up.

4. Add sesame oil and stir. Add salt and pepper. Taste rice and adjust seasoning as you like.

5. Turn heat to low and cover while you fry your eggs.

6. After eggs are fried, divide rice evenly into four bowls. Top with fried eggs and a sprinkling of scallions.

1 cup red lentils

2 tablespoons vegetable oil or butter

1 teaspoon mustard seed

2 tablespoons fresh ginger, peeled and finely chopped

5 cloves of garlic, peeled and finely minced

2 onions, roughly chopped

3 serrano peppers, seeded and finely minced

1 tablespoon ground coriander

1 tablespoon ground cumin

4 tomatoes, seeded and roughly chopped

Salt and pepper, to taste

2 tablespoons fresh cilantro leaves, finely chopped

Dahl

A hearty dish that will have your kitchen nice and fragrant. Serve with rice and garnish with chopped fresh chilies for extra spice.

1. Cook the lentils. Place them in a large pot and cover them with salted water. Bring to a boil, then reduce heat and let simmer until tender, about 20 minutes.

2. Drain lentils, but reserve their cooking water.

3. In a skillet over medium-high heat, heat the oil or butter. Add the mustard seeds and cook until they begin to dance around in the pan.

4. Add ginger, garlic, onions, and serrano peppers. Sauté until the onions and garlic are golden brown, about 5 minutes.

5. Add coriander and cumin and stir. Add chopped tomatoes. Sauté mixture until the tomatoes are softened and well-cooked, 6–8 minutes.

6. Add 1 cup reserved lentil cooking water to skillet, bring to boil and lower heat. Add cooked lentils and stir to combine. Add salt and pepper to taste and let simmer another few minutes over low heat.

7. Just before you are ready to serve the dahl, take off heat and add cilantro leaves.

Dahl

Dahl (also sometimes spelled *daal* or *dal*) is a stew of lentils that is found in Indian, Nepalese, Pakistani, Sri Lankan, and Bangladeshi cuisine. The word comes from the Sanskrit word meaning *to split*. Dahl is usually accompanied by rice, vegetables, and flatbread, depending on what region or country you are in.

1 cup coconut milk

2 tablespoons fresh lemongrass, finely chopped

1 onion, peeled and quartered

4 cloves of garlic, peeled and smashed

1 (1") piece of ginger, roughly chopped

3 red chilies (jalapeño, serrano, or Fresno are good choices), roughly chopped

¾ tablespoon tamarind paste

1 tablespoon brown sugar

2 teaspoons soy sauce

4 tablespoons fish sauce

½ teaspoon turmeric

1 tablespoon ground cumin

1 tablespoon ground coriander

1 teaspoon ground cinnamon

½ teaspoon ground nutmeg

¼ teaspoon cloves

2 teaspoons shrimp paste (available at Asian markets, omit if you can't find any)

1 tablespoon vegetable oil

3 pounds beef

Indonesian Rendang Curry Beef

Yes, the list of ingredients is long, but the sauce is actually quite easy to make and packs a ridiculous amount of flavor.

1. Place all the ingredients except for the beef in a food processor. Process until it forms a thick, smooth paste. Taste and adjust seasoning to your liking. (Add more chili for spice, more salt, etc.)

2. Heat 1 tablespoon of vegetable oil in a wok or large skillet. Add sauce and stir-fry until fragrant, about 2 minutes.

3. Add beef and stir to coat. Bring to a boil and then reduce heat and let simmer until beef is tender and sauce is very thick, about 45–60 minutes.

4. Serve hot with white rice.

Rendang Curry

Rendang is a "dry" curry, which means that the sauce is simmered down until it is essentially a thick paste. Because it's cooked for so long, the flavor becomes extra rich and concentrated. And, because it's so thick, it coats the meat in layers and layers of flavor.

CHAPTER 16

Pickled and Preserved Peppers

1 pound fresh jalapeño peppers, washed

2½ cups water

2½ cups white vinegar

3 tablespoons kosher salt

1 tablespoon sugar

4 garlic cloves, peeled and thinly sliced

2 tablespoons coriander seeds

2 tablespoons black peppercorns

2 bay leaves

Vinegar Pickled Peppers

You can use this basic brine for any kind of chili pepper. You could also use it for any vegetable, just add a few sliced chilies and a pinch of red pepper flakes for spicy pickles.

1. With a small paring knife, poke each pepper 2 or 3 times, creating small slits for the brine to seep in. Put peppers in a large, clean glass preserving jar or several smaller ones.

2. In a nonreactive sauce pan, combine all remaining ingredients and bring to a boil. Reduce heat and let simmer for 2 minutes.

3. Remove brine from heat and pour over peppers. Screw the lid onto the jars and let cool.

4. When peppers are cool, put jars in the refrigerator and let sit for several days. You can eat them after just a few days, but they will taste better if you let them sit for at least a week.

Pickling Spices

For extra flavor in your pickles, experiment with other spices you like from your pantry. Good options for pickling spices include: dried chilies, cinnamon sticks, mustard seeds, dill seeds, fennel seeds, allspice, cloves, and star anise. The best tasting pickles are the ones that you create to suit your own preferences.

1 pound fresh red jalapeño chilies, washed

⅓ cup kosher salt

Salt Pickled Peppers

This simple recipe works best with fresh red chilies because the salt preserves their bright color and makes them especially striking. Feel free to use whatever kind of chilies you like, and consider adding other vegetables to the mix.

1. Make sure your chilies are thoroughly dried. Cut off the stems and tips and roughly chop them, keeping the seeds. It's a good idea to wear gloves for this task to avoid chili burns, as you'll be handling quite a few chilies.

2. Place the chopped chilies in a large bowl. Add the salt and mix thoroughly.

3. Place chilies in a large, clean glass jar or several smaller ones. Feel free to pack them to the top, as they will shrink in size. Fill in any excess space at the top with more salt.

4. Screw lids on tightly and leave in a cool place for 2 weeks before using. Once opened, store chilies in the refrigerator for several months.

Salt Pickles

When most people think of pickles, they think of vegetables floating in a vinegary brine. But pickles do not require vinegar and in much of the world, preserving is done simply with salt. Salt draws the moisture out of vegetables, which are made mostly of water, leaving behind crisp pickles with a clean, pure flavor.

12 pickling cucumbers (also called kirbys), cut lengthwise into quarters

2 serrano peppers, thinly sliced

2 cups white vinegar

1½ cups water

1 tablespoon coriander seeds

1 tablespoon black peppercorns

1 teaspoon fennel seeds

1 teaspoon crushed red chili pepper flakes

1 bunch dill, roughly chopped

Spicy Dill Pickles

A hotter take on the classic American dill pickle. Feel free to turn up the heat as you like.

1. Combine all ingredients except dill in a large bowl. Stir and let sit at room temperature for at least 2 hours.

2. Divide dill evenly into 2 or 3 jars. Divide cucumber spears evenly into jars as well.

3. Pour pickling liquid over cucumber spears.

4. Screw lids on and store in the refrigerator for 2 days before using.

INGREDIENTS | YIELDS 8 CUPS

½ head green cabbage, thinly shredded

10 jalapeño peppers, finely chopped (take out seeds and ribs for less heat)

3 red bell peppers, seeded and chopped

3 green bell peppers, seeded and chopped

3 green tomatoes, chopped

2 sweet onions, chopped

⅓ cup kosher salt

2 cups vinegar

1 cup sugar

2 teaspoons celery seed

2 teaspoons fennel seed

2 teaspoons mustard seed

2 teaspoons turmeric

Spicy Chow Chow

This sweet and spicy relish is a Southern favorite. Try it on hamburgers, hot dogs, or alongside a meal with mashed potatoes.

1. In a large bowl, combine cabbage, jalapeños, peppers, tomatoes, and onions. Add the salt and stir well to combine. Cover and refrigerate for 6–8 hours, then rinse and drain well in a colander.

2. Put the vegetables into a large Dutch oven. Add the vinegar, sugar, celery, fennel, mustard, and turmeric. Bring to a boil then reduce heat and simmer until vegetables are tender but not falling apart, about 1 hour.

3. Remove vegetables and let cool. Place in jars and store in the refrigerator for 2 weeks.

Chow Chow

Chow Chow is mainly known as a Southern food, though a sweeter version of it is also found in Pennsylvania. It wasn't always Southern, though. Chow Chow migrated with the Acadian people after they were banished from Nova Scotia and settled in Louisiana.

Spicy Pickled Eggs

These may sound a little odd, but they are delicious. Try them on their own as an appetizer or sliced on top of crackers or bread. Pickled eggs were once a popular bar snack, so crack a beer while you're at it.

INGREDIENTS | YIELDS 6 EGGS

6 eggs

1 tablespoon kosher salt

2 fresh green serrano peppers, sliced

3 garlic cloves, peeled and thinly sliced

1½ cups apple cider vinegar

½ cup water

1 teaspoon black peppercorns

1 teaspoon coriander seeds

2 whole cloves

½ teaspoon allspice

1. Hard boil the eggs by placing them in a single layer at the bottom of a pot and covering with cold water. Bring to a boil over medium-high, then immediately remove pot from heat and cover with lid. Let sit 12 minutes, then drain and rinse with cool water.

2. When eggs are cool enough to handle, peel them. Using a fork, gently pierce each egg through to the yolk 4 times. Place the eggs in a large, clean glass preserving jar or two smaller ones.

3. In a nonreactive saucepan, combine the remaining ingredients. Bring to a boil, then reduce heat and let simmer for 10–15 minutes. Remove from heat and let cool for a few minutes.

4. Carefully pour warm mixture over the eggs.

5. Screw the lids onto jars and refrigerate for 1 week before using. Pickled eggs will keep in the refrigerator for several weeks.

1 tablespoon sugar

1 cup apple cider vinegar

2 bay leaves

1 teaspoon coriander seeds

1 teaspoon mustard seeds

1 red onion, thinly sliced

4 garlic cloves, peeled and thinly sliced

4 Scotch bonnet chilies, stem, seeds and ribs removed, horizontally and thinly sliced (use habaneros if you can't find Scotch bonnets)

4 jalapeño peppers, seeds and ribs removed, thinly sliced

2 small carrots (or 1 large) thinly sliced

2 cups rum (preferably dark rum)

Rum Chilies

Try these on top of fish for a little spicy, Caribbean flair. Be sure to use gloves when handling the extremely spicy Scotch bonnet chilies.

1. In a nonreactive saucepan, combine sugar, vinegar, bay leaves, coriander, and mustard. Bring to a boil, then reduce heat and let simmer for 5 minutes. Remove from heat and let cool.

2. Place onions, garlic, chilies, and carrots in a large, clean glass preserving jar or several smaller ones.

3. When the vinegar mixture has cooled, but is still warm, add the rum. Stir to combine, then pour mixture over chilies.

4. Screw lids on jars and store in the refrigerator for a few days before using.

Preserving in Alcohol

Besides salt and vinegar, you can also preserve or "pickle" chilies in alcohol. Using alcohol is one of the simplest methods of preserving because it kills bacteria. Alcohols like rum have a high sugar content so they will give the chili peppers sweetness as well. Try it with vodka, gin, tequila, or even whiskey.

1 head of Napa cabbage (about 2 pounds)

6 tablespoons kosher salt

1 daikon radish (look for a smaller daikon), cut into thin matchsticks

2 tablespoons ground Korean red chilies (you should be able to find this at most Asian groceries, if not use red chili pepper flakes)

2 tablespoons sugar

4 cloves of garlic, peeled and finely minced

½ bunch scallions, finely chopped

1 (2") piece of fresh ginger root, peeled and finely minced

4 tablespoons fish sauce, available at Asian markets

3 tablespoons salted shrimp paste (optional, available at Asian markets)

Quick Kimchi

Kimchi, a staple of Korean cuisine, is potent, funky, fiery, and probably not for everyone. It's often fermented for weeks or months, but this quick version takes less time and is a good introduction for the kimchi curious.

1. Slicing lengthwise, cut the cabbage into quarters. Working carefully, sprinkle the quarters with salt, being sure to get salt in between all the layers of leaves.

2. Toss daikon with salt in a large bowl. Add cabbage and let vegetables sit for at least 2 hours.

3. After a few hours, the cabbage should be quite wilted. Put cabbage and daikon in a colander to drain liquid. Rinse well, making sure to get all the salt out from in between the leaves. Shake gently to dry.

4. Combine the rest of the ingredients into a paste, making sure to avoid inhaling peppers or rubbing your eyes and mouth while handling the paste.

5. Rub the paste all over the vegetables, again getting inside all of the layers of cabbage leaves. Pack the kimchi into a large, clean glass preserving jar or several smaller ones. You may need to cut the cabbage into smaller sections to do so.

6. Screw the lid on the jars and let kimchi sit out for 24 hours before refrigerating.

7. Move kimchi to the refrigerator, using as needed. It will continue to ferment in the refrigerator, getting even tastier and more sour. It will keep for at least a week.

Indian Mixed Pickles

INGREDIENTS | YIELDS ABOUT 2 CUPS OF PICKLES

1 cup cauliflower, cut into small florets

2 shallots, cut horizontally into thin slices

1 large carrot, cut into thin strips

4 green jalapeño peppers, seeds and ribs removed, sliced lengthwise

1 thumb-sized piece of fresh ginger, peeled and sliced into thin matchsticks

1 teaspoon salt

½ teaspoon cayenne pepper

½ teaspoon ground turmeric

3 teaspoons fresh lime juice

2 teaspoons mustard seeds

1 teaspoon fenugreek seeds

¼ cup vegetable oil

These tangy, spicy pickles are traditionally served alongside most Indian meals. Try them on their own or with flatbread.

1. Mix all the vegetables together in a large, nonreactive bowl with salt, cayenne, turmeric, and lime juice. Set aside

2. In a spice grinder, blend mustard and fenugreek seeds into a fine powder. Add to vegetables and stir to combine.

3. Pack vegetables into a clean glass preserving jar. Add oil.

4. Screw lid on jar and place in the refrigerator. Let sit for 2–3 days before using.

Fenugreek

Fenugreek is a plant that can be used both as a spice (the seed) and an herb (the leaves). Fenugreek is used throughout Indian and South Asian cuisine, as well as in Ethiopian and Eritrean cooking. It adds an earthy flavor to curries and sauces and can be found in most Indian and Middle Eastern markets.

3 ripe yellow mangoes, peeled, pitted, and cut into ½" cubes

1 (2") piece fresh ginger, peeled and finely minced

2 garlic cloves, peeled and finely minced

½ teaspoon salt

½ teaspoon cayenne pepper

1 cup vinegar

¾ cup light brown sugar

Mango Chutney

Sweet, sour, and spicy all at once, this chutney is great spread onto crackers, or served with fish or chicken.

1. Combine all the ingredients together in a heavy-bottomed saucepan and let simmer over very low heat for 20–30 minutes, until it is very thick.

2. Remove chutney from heat and let cool.

3. When chutney is cooled, transfer to a glass jar and store, covered, in the refrigerator for several weeks.

Green Coriander Chutney

INGREDIENTS | YIELDS ABOUT 1 CUP

1 bunch coriander (cilantro), stems included

3 or 4 sprigs of fresh mint

2 serrano chilies, seeded and roughly chopped

3 garlic cloves, peeled and roughly chopped

¼ cup unsweetened grated coconut

1 (1") piece of fresh ginger, peeled and chopped

Juice of 2 fresh lemons

½ teaspoon salt

This bright green chutney gets an extra pop from the addition of grated coconut. It's particularly good on seafood, but very nice simply spread on toast.

1. Place all the ingredients in a blender or food processor and blend until it is smooth.

2. Pour chutney into a jar. It may seem a little thin, but will thicken into a paste.

3. Store in the refrigerator where it will keep for up to 1 month.

Chutney

Chutneys are condiments and spreads made from cooking down fruit that is flavored with spices. The word comes from the Hindi *catni* and originated as a South Asian food, though now it is used and made around the world. Chutneys can be made from almost any fruit or vegetable, but common ones found are mango, tomato, and tamarind.

CHAPTER 17

Hot and Sweet:
Desserts and Drinks

Pineapple, peeled, cored, and cut into
cubes

Mangoes, peeled, cored, and cut into
cubes

Watermelon, skin removed, cut into cubes

Papaya, peeled, cored, and cut into cubes

Jicama, peeled and cut into cubes

Fresh lime juice, to taste

Chili powder, to taste

Salt, to taste

Spicy Fruit Salad

Tropical fruit sprinkled with chili powder is a popular street snack in Mexico. Consider this a basic guide, and use any amount and combination of fruits that you like. It's impossible to screw this up.

1. Place all the fruit in a large, shallow bowl.

2. Squeeze lime juice all over the fruit. Sprinkle generously with chili powder, then sprinkle with salt.

3. Stir the fruit gently to mix ingredients without bruising fruit.

4. Taste and adjust seasoning to your liking.

Jicama

Jicama (pronounced "hee-ka-MA") is a common Mexican ingredient. It's a root vegetable that has a thin brown skin and a crunchy white flesh. It has a mild flavor that is both sweet and earthy. It can be eaten raw or cooked, but when used raw it adds a refreshing crunch and snap to dishes like salad.

8 large mangoes, peeled, pitted, and cut into small cubes

2 cups sugar

¾ cup fresh lime juice

½ teaspoon ancho chili powder

Mango Chili Sorbet

Based on the Mexican fruit with chili snack, this nondairy ice frozen treat is perfect on a hot day. For ultra-smooth ice, purée the mixture 2 or 3 times. Or just enjoy it chunky.

1. Put all ingredients in a blender and process until smooth. You may need to add just a little bit of water.

2. Pour mixture into large bowl. Cover and put in freezer for 2 hours.

3. Take the mixture out of the freezer and purée in blender again.

4. Freeze mixture again until solid. Serve with an extra sprinkling of chili powder.

Mangoes

Mangoes are a tropical fruit than have been cultivated since as far back as 2,000 B.C. in India. Today, they are cultivated throughout Southeast Asia, Mexico, South America, and the Caribbean. Because they continue to ripen even after they are picked, mangoes are a popular export crop and have no trouble making long journeys to their final destinations.

1 cup whole milk

2 cups heavy cream

¾ cup granulated sugar

1 cinnamon stick

6 egg yolks

½ teaspoon ground cayenne pepper

Red Chili Ice Cream

The ice cream may be cold, but the cayenne pepper and cinnamon in it will give your tongue an unmistakably warm feeling. The heat level here is mild to medium, but feel free to punch it up by adding even more chili pepper.

1. In a medium, heavy-bottomed saucepan, combine milk, heavy cream, sugar, and cinnamon stick. Heat until scalding, then remove from heat, cover, and let mixture infuse for one hour.

2. In a bowl, stir together the egg yolks.

3. Remove the cinnamon stick from the milk and rewarm the milk at a low temperature. Gradually pour some of the milk into the egg yolks, whisking constantly. Return the warmed yolks and milk back to the saucepan.

4. Add the cayenne pepper and cook mixture over low heat, stirring constantly. Scrape the bottom of the pan as you stir, heating until the custard is thick enough to coat the back of a spoon.

5. Remove mixture from heat and let cool completely. Place the mixture in the refrigerator to chill thoroughly, overnight if possible.

6. After mixture is cooled, freeze it in your ice cream maker according to the manufacturer's instructions.

INGREDIENTS | SERVES 4

4 cups whole milk

½ cup water

8 ounces bittersweet chocolate, finely chopped (you could also use chocolate chips)

2 tablespoons sugar

1 teaspoon vanilla extract

½ teaspoon chili powder

¼ teaspoon ground cinnamon

Pinch of kosher salt

Mexican Hot Chocolate

Few things are a more comforting on a winter night than a cup of hot cocoa, except this hot cocoa with a little extra spice.

1. Over medium heat, combine all the ingredients in a large saucepan. Whisk constantly until mixture is hot, but not boiling, about 6–8 minutes.

2. Pour into mugs.

The Skinny on Whole Milk

Whole milk, 2%, 1%, and skim—what's the difference? These numbers and names refer to the amount of fat that is found in the milk. While calling it *whole* makes it seem like it's made entirely of fat, the truth is it is about 3.5 percent milk fat. Obviously, 2% and 1%, contain those amounts of fat, respectively. The difference is not that big on the calorie front either, with one 8-ounce serving of whole milk containing about 146 calories, while 2% holds 122, 1% holds 102, and skim containing 86.

4 ounces bittersweet chocolate, roughly chopped

1 stick unsalted butter, softened, and cut into little cubes

1 cup sugar

2 eggs

½ teaspoon vanilla extract

¼ cup bourbon

½ cup plus 1 tablespoon all-purpose flour

⅛ teaspoon salt

¼ teaspoon cinnamon

½ teaspoon ancho chili powder

Bourbon and Chili Brownies

This recipe yields dense, chewy brownies with spicy hints of chili and bourbon.

1. Heat the oven to 350°F. Grease an 8" square baking pan.

2. Combine chocolate and butter in a small, microwavable bowl. Microwave 20 seconds at a time until they are melted, stir until smooth. (You can also melt the chocolate and butter in a small saucepan on the stove.)

3. Transfer chocolate mixture to a large bowl. Add sugar and stir to combine.

4. Add eggs, one at a time, stirring after each until smooth.

5. Add vanilla extract and bourbon, then stir.

6. Add flour, salt, cinnamon, and chili powder. Stir gently until smooth.

7. Pour mixture into baking pan and bake 20–25 minutes, until they are just set in the middle and a toothpick stuck in comes out clean.

8. Let brownies cool before cutting.

1 tablespoon heavy cream

1 tablespoon dark rum

¼ teaspoon Tabasco sauce

1 cup pecan halves

¼ cup brown sugar

Louisiana Praline Pecans

These sweet tidbits are made from whole individual (shelled) pecans with a rum praline coating on each one.

1. Preheat oven to 350°F.

2. Combine the cream, rum, and Tabasco in a bowl. Add the pecans and stir to coat. Add the brown sugar and toss with a fork to coat the pecans.

3. Pour the coated pecans onto a baking sheet lined with nonstick foil and separate them into individual nuts with a fork.

4. Bake for 10 minutes, stir the nuts around, and bake another 5 minutes. Let cool on the foil and then store in a tin with a tight-fitting lid.

Rum and Sugar

Most anywhere sugarcane grows rum is made, because rum is made from sugarcane. This includes the Caribbean. Jamaican rum is dark and slightly sweet, and Puerto Rican rum is lighter and drier. Whether the rum is dark, gold, white, or spiced, it is usually 80 proof, which means it is 40 percent alcohol. The exception is 151 rum, which is 75.5 percent alcohol. Beware!

4 cups milk

2 (3-ounce) packages instant vanilla pudding mix

3 bananas

1 tablespoon lime juice

¼ teaspoon ground ancho chili powder

⅛ teaspoon cayenne pepper

1 cup whipped cream

2 cups mini semisweet chocolate chips

18 paper drink cups

18 frozen-dessert sticks

Spicy Banana Pops

An easy, mix and freeze dessert that spices up a classic combo of bananas and chocolate. Add as much or as little cayenne as you like.

1. In large bowl, combine milk and pudding mixes and beat with wire whisk until thickened.

2. In small bowl, mash bananas with lime juice and stir into pudding mixture.

3. Add chili powder, cayenne pepper, and fold in whipped cream and mini chocolate chips.

4. Divide mixture evenly among paper drink cups.

5. Place drink cups on baking sheet and freeze for 1–2 hours until just firm. Insert frozen-dessert sticks into banana mixture, return to freezer, and freeze for 3–4 hours until frozen solid. Peel away drink cups to serve.

2 (46-ounce) cans tomato juice

Juice of 2 fresh lemons

2 tablespoons Worcestershire sauce

1 tablespoon horseradish

¼ teaspoon cayenne pepper

½ teaspoon celery salt

½ teaspoon ground black pepper

Tabasco (or any hot sauce of your liking) to taste

Bloody Mary Mix

Instead of having to make the same drink over and over again, make a batch of this Bloody Mary mix before having people over for brunch.

Mix all ingredients and refrigerate. You can add many types of ingredients to a basic Bloody Mary mix: raw horseradish, lime juice, A1 steak sauce, wasabi, chili powder, bitters, or anything else you like. Go wild. Combine 2 cups Bloody Mary mix with 1–2 shots of vodka to make a Bloody Mary.

2 lime wedges

¼ teaspoon celery salt

¼ teaspoon Worcestershire sauce

⅛ teaspoon pepper

1 dash of Tabasco sauce

1 ounce tequila

5 ounces tomato juice

Bloody Maria

The Bloody Mary goes south-of-the-border with tequila and lime instead of vodka and a celery stalk.

1. Run a lime wedge around the rim of a tall glass, then dip the rim in celery salt.

2. Fill the glass with ice and squeeze the same lime wedge into it.

3. Shake the celery salt, Worcestershire sauce, pepper, and Tabasco sauce into the glass.

4. Add the tequila and tomato juice and stir well with a long iced tea or bar spoon. Garnish with a lime wedge.

1 (16-ounce) bottle beer

2 tablespoons lime juice

¼ teaspoon Tabasco sauce

2 teaspoons Worcestershire sauce

1 tablespoon soy sauce

½ teaspoon salt

2 cups crushed ice

Micheladas

You can vary the ingredients in this classic Mexican drink to your taste. Try it with different kinds of beer too; dark ale will make a more robust Michelada than a light beer.

In a cocktail shaker, combine all ingredients except ice and shake to blend well. Strain over ice.

In the Liquor Store

In some liquor stores or grocery stores, you may be able to find a Michelada mix to add to cold beer. Or you could use Clamato, a tomato-based liquid that contains clam juice. But the real fun lies in experimenting and adjusting the spices to your liking.

2 cucumbers

⅓ cup lime juice

2 tablespoons superfine sugar

½ cup tequila

½ teaspoon salt

¼ teaspoon cayenne pepper

1 cup crushed ice

Cucumber Margaritas

Cucumbers offer a mild and cooling contrast in these pretty light green drinks.

1. Peel cucumber, cut in half, and remove seeds with a spoon. Cut into chunks and place in blender container or food processor with remaining ingredients. Cover and blend or process until mixture is smooth and thick.

2. Serve immediately, garnished with cucumber slices.

INGREDIENTS | YIELDS 1 SHOT

1½ ounces tequila

Several dashes Tabasco

⅛ ounce 151 rum

Hot Blooded

Be very careful when lighting this on fire. It's all fun until somebody gets their face burned.

Pour the tequila into a shot glass and add several dashes of Tabasco. Gently layer the 151 rum on top, then light. Allow the flame to die out, then drink.

Flaming Shots

There is a common misconception that lighting a shot on fire concentrates the liquor and makes the drink stronger. In reality, lighting the liquor on fire makes the drink less strong. The fire burns away the alcohol and weakens the drink.

1½ ounces tequila

3 dashes Tabasco

Prairie Fire Shooter

One taste and you'll understand why they call it fire. You can chase the shooter with a beer to calm the fire.

Pour tequila into a shot glass and add the Tabasco.

Tequila

Tequila is made form the blue agave, a cactus-like plant that grows in the area near the city of Tequila. True tequila must have a blue agave content of 51 percent, otherwise it is called mezdal. Fine tequilas are 100 percent blue agave.

1 ounce reposado tequila

1 ounce blanco tequila

1 ounce Clamato juice

1 ounce fresh lime juice

¼ ounce Tabasco

Kosher salt

Dynamite

Two of these and you'll be running through the house shouting, "Dy-no-MITE!"

Rim a short glass with kosher salt. Fill the glass with ice, and pour all ingredients in.

Clamato

As its name indicates, Clamato is a tomato-based juice that also contains clam juice and other spices. It's been around since the 1960s, and was first produced by the Duffy-Mott corporation. Now, Clamato is part of the international Cadbury Schweppes empire, the people famous for making Easter candy and ginger ale.

6 ounces Clamato juice

1 ounce fresh lime juice

¼ teaspoon horseradish

Dash Tabasco sauce

Dash Worcestershire sauce

1 lemon wedge

Hot Clamato

Here's a mocktail with a kick.

Pour ingredients into a glass over ice; stir. Garnish with lemon.

APPENDIX A

Additional Resources

Websites

Bon Appetit's 25 Ways to Use Sriracha
A terrific online slideshow illustrating simple ways to use Sriracha.
www.bonappetit.com/recipes/slideshows/2011/06/sriracha-recipes-slideshow

The Chile Man
A great site for learning how to grow chilies.
www.thechileman.org

The Cook's Thesaurus Chili Guide
A nice and basic guide to common fresh chilies, including substitution guides.
www.foodsubs.com/Chilefre.html

Hot Sauce World
A vast, online shop filled with hundreds of bottled hot sauces.
www.hotsauceworld.com

Huy Fong Foods, Inc.
The company website for the people behind Sriracha, with a few recipes.
www.huyfong.com

Tabasco.com
The Tabasco brand website, with over 1,000 recipes.
www.tabasco.com

World Spice Merchants
An amazing selection of dried chilies, chili powders, and hard-to-find spices and spice blends.
www.worldspice.com

Books

Bayless, Rick. *Rick Bayless's Mexican Kitchen.* (New York, NY: Scribner, 1996).

Kennedy, Diana. *The Art of Mexican Cooking.* (New York, NY: Clarkson Potter, 2008).

Samuelsson, Marcus. *The Soul of a New Cuisine.* (Hoboken, NJ: John Wiley & Songs, 2006).

Viestad, Andreas. *Where Flavor Was Born: Recipes and Culinary Travels Along the Indian Ocean Spice Route.* (San Francisco, CA: Chronicle Books, 2007).

APPENDIX B

Food Preparation Glossary

additives

Strictly regulated ingredients and chemicals added to food to help improve texture and flavor and to extend the shelf life of products.

al dente

Italian term that translates to "to the tooth." *Al dente* is used to describe the state to which pasta should be cooked. Pasta that is cooked al dente has no taste of flour remaining, but there is still a slight resistance when bitten and it is still slightly chewy.

Ancho chilies

Ripe, red poblano chilies that have been dried.

antibacterials

Compounds that destroy or prevent the growth of bacteria, they can kill both harmful and good bacteria.

antioxidants

Substances or nutrients in food that can slow or prevent oxidation in the body. Plant foods, especially those that are darkly colored or strongly flavored provide a good source of antioxidants.

apex

The bottom tip or blossom end of the chili pepper.

aromatics

When cooking, garlic and ginger are frequently added to the hot oil before the other ingredients, in order to flavor the oil.

ascorbic acid

An organic acid also known as vitamin C. It is used to help prevent enzymatic browning in fruits and vegetables.

baking powder

A leavening agent used in baked goods that combines an acid and a base to produce carbon dioxide when mixed with water. The carbon dioxide fills small bubbles in the batter or dough and expands when baked to form the characteristic crumb.

baking soda

Bicarbonate of soda is used as a leavening agent in baked goods. It combines with an acidic ingredient in the dough or batter to produce carbon dioxide so the product expands while baking.

baste

To spoon or pour a liquid over foods during cooking to help glaze food and prevent drying.

batter

A combination of flour and liquid mixed together by stirring or beating to form a pourable mass.

beat

To rapidly stir a batter with force to incorporate dry and wet ingredients. Beating also incorporates air into the batter or dough.

blanch

To dip foods, especially fruits and vegetables, into boiling water for a brief period. The blanched food is then plunged into ice water to stop the cooking process. Foods are blanched before freezing to set the color, so the skin will slip off, and to stop enzymatic reactions.

blend

To stir or gently mix several ingredients together until the separate ingredients are no longer visible.

blind bake

To bake a pie shell without a filling. Pie crusts that are blind baked are usually lined with foil and filled with pie weights or dried beans to stop the dough from puffing.

boil

To raise the temperature of a liquid to 212°F or 100°C so that bubbles rise from the bottom of the liquid to the top and break on the surface.

bone

To remove the bone from meat or fish. A piece of meat that has major bones removed is called partially boned.

braise

To cook meat in a liquid environment for long periods of time to melt connective tissue and tenderize the product. This wet-heat method of cooking is used on less tender cuts of meat.

broil

To cook food a few inches away from a burner or flame turned to its highest point. This dry-heat method of cooking can be done in an oven or over a grill.

brown

To cook over high heat so the exterior turns color to a deep brown while the interior remains uncooked or undercooked.

bulgur

Whole wheat kernels that have been parboiled, dried and crushed. Bulgur is used in pilaf and tabouli.

calyx

Also called the crown, is the remnant of the flower from which the chili grew.

capsaicin

The heat in chilies comes from this chemical compound. Capsaicin is produced in the capsaicin glands in the placenta of each chili pepper. Capsaicin is an alkaloid that, while lacking any distinct flavor or color, is so potent it can withstand long periods of drying, freezing, and heating or cooking without losing any of its strength.

capsicum

A genus of plants in the Nightshade family called *Solanaceae*.

Capsicum Annuums

The most common and extensively cultivated species of all chili peppers. Annuums run the gamut from bell peppers to milder peppers like jalapeño, Anaheim, poblano, New Mexico, and Hungarian wax.

Capsicum Baccatum

The name *baccatum* refers to the small berry-like fruits that flourished in this species' wild chilies.

Capsicum Chinense

Species of peppers that includes some extremely hot peppers such as habaneros, Scotch bonnets, and Ghost Peppers—Chinense peppers are not for the faint of heart or the weak-tongued.

Capsicum Frutescens

Species of peppers that are typically small and quite spicy.

Capsicum Pubescens

Peppers from the capsicum pubescens species are not very well known outside of Central and South America. The name *pubescens* refers to the hairs that grow on the underside of the plant's leaves. The fruits are thick-skinned, like bell peppers, and apple shaped.

Cascabels

Small, round chilies with dark reddish brown skin.

chickpeas

Chickpeas are also known as garbanzo beans and are common in the Mediterranean, West Asia, and India. Chickpeas are good in salads but are most commonly found in hummus and falafel.

chili (chili pepper)

The fruit of any *capsicum* plant, often called by their more official and scientific name: *capsicums*.

chiles de arbol

Long, skinny chiles begin green, but ripen to a solid red, which fades slightly after they are dried. Chiles de arbol are very hot with a distinct, pleasantly bitter flavor.

chipotle

Possibly the most famous dried chili outside of Mexico, which is appropriate since it is really a jalapeño, one of the most recognized peppers in the world. Chipotles are simply red, ripened jalapeños that are and smoked and dried.

chop

To cut in roughly uniform bite-size pieces with a sharp knife. Chopped food is in larger pieces than minced or diced food.

chunk

To cut food into large, thick pieces. Chunked carrots, for example, are cut into 3 to 4 pieces per carrot.

complex carbohydrates

Chains of three or more simple sugars linked together. There are two types of complex carbohydrates, starches and cellulose. Complex carbohydrates are digested more slowly than simple sugars and are found in vegetables, grains, nuts, seeds, and beans.

couscous

A small-grain semolina, or granular wheat, common in Middle Eastern cooking. Couscous is actually a tiny pasta, not a whole grain.

cream

To combine a fat and a dry ingredient together until a smooth mass forms. Creaming helps develop the crumb of a baked good, since sugar crystals make tiny holes in the fat.

crepe

A very thin, delicate pancake of French origin that is used in both dessert and savory dishes.

cruciferous

Cruciferous vegetables come from the Brassica family of vegetables. The cruciferous name, in Latin *Crucifer*, reflects the four sections of the plant that appear in the shape of a cross. They are sulfur-containing vegetables, which is why they all have a strong taste.

crumb

The texture of a baked good. A fine crumb means the air holes in the product are very small. A coarse crumb means the air holes in the product are large.

cut in

To combine shortening or fat with dry ingredients using two knives or a pastry blender until particles of fat coated with dry ingredients are small and blended.

deep-fry

Deep-frying is a means of cooking food by immersing it briefly in hot oil.

deglaze

To pour liquid into a hot pan in which meat has been browned, loosening from the bottom the drippings and brown particles that form during browning.

dice

To cut with a sharp knife into small, even square pieces, about ⅛ inch to ¼ inch in diameter.

dock

To pierce tiny holes in the bottom and sides of an unbaked pie crust to help prevent puffing while the crust blind bakes.

dot

To place small bits of one ingredient on top of another. Usually butter is dotted over pie fillings or pastries.

drain

To remove the liquid from a food, usually by pouring into a strainer or colander. Some foods, such as frozen spinach, must be thoroughly drained by pressing on them with the back of a spoon to remove as much liquid as possible.

dredge

To coat food with a light layer of flour, cornstarch, or very fine crumbs.

drippings

The melted fat, juices, and browned particles left in the bottom of a pan after meat or vegetables have been browned.

drizzle

To pour a thin liquid mixture in a very fine stream over baked goods or other foods.

dry ingredients

Flour, salt, baking powder, flavorings, herbs, and other ingredients that are low in water content.

dry rub

A combination of herbs, salt, pepper, and spices that is rubbed into meats to help flavor and tenderize before cooking.

ellagic acid

A phytochemical found in raspberries, strawberries, cranberries, walnuts, pecans, pomegranates, and other plant foods. Ellagic acid acts as an antioxidant and may help reduce the risk of several forms of cancer.

enzymes

Molecules, usually proteins, found in cells that help encourage and speed up reactions between chemicals.

exocarp

The outermost layer of the pepper, the only "skin" that is visible when you look at a pepper whole.

fillet

To remove the bones, skin, and sometimes cartilage from a piece of meat, poultry, or seafood. Also a piece of meat with no bones or skin.

flake

To gently tease apart cooked meat, especially seafood, along the natural lines of separation or layers between muscles.

flash freeze

To freeze unwrapped food quickly, usually in a single layer on a cookie sheet or baking pan. Food that is flash frozen is generally small, such as balls of cookie dough or small appetizers.

flavonoids

A group of phytonutrients found in a wide variety of fruits, vegetables and tea. Flavonoids act as antioxidants, help with brain function and may keep the immune system healthy.

flute

To make a decorative border on a pie crust by using the fingers or a utensil to push a pattern into the dough.

fold

To combine two mixtures by an action of gently cutting a spoon or spatula down through the mixtures, scraping the bottom of the bowl, and turning the mixtures over until combined.

freezer burn

Food that is improperly wrapped and frozen may have dry hard patches, or freezer burn, caused by moisture evaporating in the cold climate of the freezer. Freezer burn is not dangerous, but it makes the food unpalatable.

fry

A dry-heat cooking method where the food is surrounded by hot cooking oil until it reaches a safe internal temperature.

glaze

To pour a thin coating over foods to evenly coat. A glaze is also a thin liquid that flavors foods and dries to a high gloss.

glutathione

A naturally occurring, sulfur containing antioxidant. Cruciferous vegetables are rich in glutathione

grease

To coat the surface of a baking pan or sheet with shortening, butter, or oil before adding the batter, preventing the food from sticking after it is cooked.

guajillos

Mirasol chilies that have been dried, and they have a smooth, dark red—almost purple—skin medium-to-hot level of spice.

half-and-half

A dairy product with fat content halfway between whole milk and heavy cream. Half-and-half is also called coffee cream.

head space

An air pocket deliberately left in a rigid container that allows for expansion of liquids when frozen.

homocysteine

Homocysteine is an amino acid found in the blood. Too much homocysteine is associated with an increased risk of heart disease. Folic acid, found in green, leafy vegetables and fortified grains, can help keep homocysteine levels low.

inflammation

Inflammation is a normal reaction of the body to foreign bodies or matter. Inflammation helps the body protect itself while healing occurs. Inflammation that goes on all the time, called chronic inflammation, is not a healthy process and is the cause of damage to the body leading to aging and disease. Studies show diet plays a role in triggering and eliminating inflammation.

insoluble fiber

Insoluble fiber is a group of three fibers that act together to aid regularity. Insoluble fibers do not dissolve in water but do hold onto water helping to move waste products through the intestine. They may help protect against cancer. Common fibers are wheat, corn, flax and many vegetables.

isothiocyanates

Antioxidant found in cruciferous vegetables that also helps detoxify harmful compounds in the body and can help boost antioxidant capability of cells. Found in sulphur containing foods like broccoli, cabbage, cauliflower, turnips and kale.

jelly roll pan

A large pan with 1-inch sides used to bake cakes used in jelly rolls, or for baking large sheet cakes or bars.

julienne

To julienne food (also called matchstick cutting) consists of cutting it into very thin strips about 1½ to 2 inches long, with a width and thickness of about ⅛ inch. Both meat and vegetables can be julienned.

kimchi

Korean national dish of preserved and fermented cabbage, often chili leaves are also added to kimchi.

knead

To physically manipulate dough by pushing and pulling it with your hands until it becomes smooth and resilient.

legume

Pod, such as a bean, that splits into two. The side the seed is attached to is used as food. Common legumes are black beans, navy beans, kidney beans, split peas and lentils.

lycopene

A member of the carotenoid family it helps reduce the risk of prostate cancer and may reduce the risk of heart disease. The best sources of lycopene are red fruits and vegetables like tomatoes, pink grapefruit and watermelon.

marinade

A combination of liquids, acids, and flavorings poured over foods, especially meats, to tenderize and flavor them before cooking.

marinate

To pour marinade over a food and let it stand for minutes or hours before cooking, to tenderize and flavor the food.

matchstick head

To prepare matchstick heads, julienne the food and then cut it crosswise into small cubes the approximate size of matchstick heads.

mesocarp

The thicker, fleshy middle layer of skin. The mesocarp contains the highest amount of water and provides the chili pepper with structural support. It is this layer that gives chilies their crispness.

millet

A small, round grain most commonly used in Europe, Asia and Africa. It has a mild flavor and it can be used in casseroles or cooked like rice.

mince

To cut into very small pieces with a sharp knife or food processor. Minced food is smaller than chopped or diced food.

monounsaturated fats

Types of fat that, along with polyunsaturated fats, help lower blood cholesterol when used in place of saturated fats. Monounsaturated fats are found in oils, nuts, seeds and fatty fish.

olive oil

The oil from pressed olives. Extra-virgin olive oil is from the first "cold" pressing, which uses no chemicals, and has the lowest acid content. Virgin olive oil is also a first pressing, but it has a slightly higher acid content. Olive oil is a combination of different pressings and is usually used for sautéing foods.

Omega – 3 fatty acids

Essential fats needed by the body but the body is not able to make these fats. Omega 3's must be provided by the diet with fatty fish, flaxseeds, walnuts and canola and soybean oils providing the best sources.

oxidation

Oxidation in food is the combination of air with chemicals in food cells. This process can change the color and texture of food and lead to rancid by-products.

parboil

To briefly cook foods in boiling water until partially cooked. Vegetables are usually parboiled before being frozen or stir-fried.

pare

To remove the thin skin or outer covering of fruits and vegetables with a knife or a swivel-bladed vegetable peeler.

partially cover

To place a cover on a pan or skillet, leaving a small opening for steam to pass through, helping reduce or thicken the sauce.

pasilla chilies

Chilaca chilies that have been allowed to fully ripen, after which they are dried.

peduncle

The botanical term for the stem of the chili pepper.

peel

To remove the skin or outer covering of fruits and vegetables with a knife or a swivel-bladed vegetable peeler.

pie weight

Small pebblelike object, usually made of stainless steel or ceramic materials, that is used in blind baking a pie crust to prevent shrinking and puffing.

pinch

The amount of an ingredient that can be held between the thumb and forefinger. Technically, it is about $\frac{1}{16}$ teaspoon.

placenta

The part of the pepper to which the seeds are attached.

poach

To cook meats, fruits, or vegetables in a liquid that is heated to just below a simmer. The poaching liquid, whether water, broth, or wine, will shimmer on the surface when the temperature is correct.

polenta

An Italian grain dish made from yellow or white cornmeal.

polyunsaturated fats

Fats that are chemically unstable and they are liquid at room temperature. Polyunsaturated fats are found mainly in corn, safflower, soybean, and sunflower oils. Polyunsaturated fats can help lower blood cholesterol when used in place of saturated fats.

prebiotics

Nondigestible compounds in food that help normal, healthy bacteria grow in your colon. Prebiotics aid in digestion and help prevent bloating and gas.

preheat

To turn on an appliance, whether an oven, grill, or stovetop burner, to heat to baking or cooking temperature before adding foods.

prick

To poke a food with the tines of a fork or the tip of a sharp knife. Most often, pie crusts are pricked to prevent buckling, shrinking, or puffing.

probiotics

Live microorganisms that are similar to healthy bacteria in the intestine and when consumed they act as healthy bacteria promoting overall health. Common probiotics are yogurt, fermented milk products like kefir, miso, and tempeh.

purée

To mash food or force it through a sieve, or to process it in a blender or food processor to make a smooth paste.

quinoa

A grain that is native to South America and is often referred to as the "Mother of all Grains". Quinoa is a complete protein making it a good choice for vegetarians. It cooks like rice and can be used in recipes that call for rice.

reduce

To cook a liquid at a rapid boil, removing much of the water by evaporation, until a thick sauce forms. A reduction is a sauce made by reducing liquid.

ristra

String of dried chilies, often used as decoration.

roast

A dry-heat cooking method where foods are cooked at high temperatures in an oven. Usually meats and vegetables are roasted.

roll out

To manipulate dough or pastry with a rolling pin or other round implement, flattening the dough into a thin and even round or square.

saturated fats

Fats that are chemically stable making them solid at room temperature. Common saturated fats are meat, poultry, butter, whole milk, coconut, palm, and palm kernel oils. Saturated fats can increase blood cholesterol.

sauce

A sauce is a liquid that is added to lend flavor to a dish.

sauté

To cook food in a small amount of oil or fat over fairly high heat in a short amount of time.

scald

Also known as blanch; to place a food in boiling water for a short amount of time. Scalded fruits and vegetables are usually cooked just long enough to set color or to remove peel or skin.

score

To make shallow cuts on a piece of meat or fish that allow marinade, tenderizers, and spices to penetrate the meat and add flavor.

Scoville Heat Units (SHU)

Scale to measure chili pepper heat.

sear

To heat foods at a very high heat in order to seal in juices and give color to the food. Searing is done with direct heat, as in a broiler, sauté pan, or grill.

seed (or seeded)

To remove the seeds from a chili pepper or other fruit.

shred

To cut food into thin strips with a grater or attachment on a food processor. Some foods can also be shredded with a knife or with two forks.

sift

To shake dry ingredients through a fine sifter or sieve to remove lumps, to combine them, and to make them lighter.

simmer

To cook food in liquid at a temperature just below a boil. Small bubbles rise to the surface and barely break when the liquid is at the proper temperature.

skewer

A long, thin piece of metal or wood used to hold food in a single row while cooking.

slice

To cut a food using a knife or food processor to make very thin strips or sections.

soften

To make a food softer, either by soaking it in water, letting it stand at room temperature, or heating it briefly. Gelatin is softened in water; butter is softened by microwaving.

soluble fiber

Soluble fiber dissolves in water to form a gel-like compound making it a good fiber to help lower cholesterol. Soluble fiber is found in high amounts in beans, barley, flaxseeds, oats, oranges, and other fruits and vegetables

Sriracha

Pronounced "sree-RA-sha". Sriracha (aka "Rooster Sauce") is produced by the Huy Fong Foods company. Its founder David Tran crafted a new hot sauce, a combination of fresh red jalapeños, garlic, sugar, salt, and vinegar.

steam

To cook food suspended over boiling water so the steam penetrates the food. Since the water doesn't come in contact with the food, steamed foods retain more nutrients and flavor than poached or simmered foods do.

stir-fry

To cook piece of food over very high heat in a skillet or wok while moving the food constantly around the pan. Foods for stir-frying are cut into similar shapes and sizes so they cook evenly.

strain

To remove large pieces of foods from a liquid or a purée using a fine mesh strainer or colander lined with cheesecloth.

sulfides

Sulfides are a group of phytonutrients found in vegetables and fruits. Sulfides are also referred to as thiols and common sulfides are garlic, onion, leeks, scallions, and cruciferous vegetables.

Tabasco

Arguably the most famous hot sauce around the world, Tabasco has been produced since 1868. It is still produced in its original location on Avery Island, Louisiana by the family-owned business, the McIlhenny Company, founded by Edmund McIlhenny. McIlhenny mashed crushed red peppers with refined Avery Island salt and aged the mixture for thirty days. He then added white wine vinegar, let the mixture age for another month, strained it and packaged it in small corked bottles.

tart

A pie, usually baked in a tart pan, which has very shallow, straight sides and a removable bottom. Tarts can be large or bite-size, filled with savory or sweet fillings.

tear

To rip or break foods, usually greens or herbs, into irregular pieces.

tinola

One of the national dishes of the Philippines, tinola is a light soup made with chicken broth, ginger, chayote squash, and chili leaves, which give the dish a distinct aroma and flavor.

toast

To brown foods over or under direct heat, whether in a dry saucepan, a broiler, or a toaster.

toss

To turn food pieces over and under each other to combine. Usually salads and other vegetable mixtures are tossed.

water bath

A large container filled either with ice water or very hot water that smaller containers of food can be placed into. This method is used to cool food quickly (using an ice-water bath) or warm it gently (using a hot-water bath).

wrap

To fold something over another ingredient. A wrap is also a sandwich that uses a flat bread such as a tortilla to hold the filling ingredients.

yeast

A single-celled organism that is preserved, usually by drying, and that multiplies when mixed with water and a food source. Yeast is used to give raised bread its characteristic crumb and flavor.

APPENDIX C

Equivalents Chart

▼ **COMMONLY USED COOKING EQUIVALENTS**

INGREDIENT	EQUIVALENT
1 pound lean ground beef	2½ cups cooked, drained
1 pound ham	3 cups cubed
8 slices bacon	½ cup cooked, drained, crumbled
1 whole chicken	3–4 cups cooked, cubed meat
1½ pounds boneless, skinless chicken breast	3 cups cooked, diced
1½ pounds beef roast	3 cups cooked, cubed
1 pound lamb chops	2 chops
1 pound onions	3 cups chopped
1 bell pepper, chopped	1 cup
3 ounces button mushrooms	1 cup sliced
1 medium cabbage	5 cups shredded
2 ribs celery	1 cup sliced
1 medium apple	1 cup chopped
1 pound apples	3 medium
3 medium bananas	1 cup mashed
1 medium tomato	1 cup chopped
1 orange	5–6 tablespoons juice
1 lemon	2–4 tablespoons juice
1 lime	1½–2 tablespoons juice
1 pound potatoes	4–5 cups chopped
1 pound broccoli	2 cups florets
1 pound carrots	2½ cups sliced
1 pound cauliflower	3 cups chopped
1 pound cranberries	4 cups
1 pound fennel bulb	3 cups sliced
1 pound grapes	2½ cups seedless
1 pound melon	1 cup diced
1 medium head lettuce	4–6 cups torn
1 pound fresh spinach	¾ cup cooked, drained
1 pint strawberries	2 cups sliced
1 pound sweet potatoes	2 large, 2 cups cubed
8 ounces (2 cups) uncooked noodles	4 cups cooked, drained
1 pound rice, 2¼ cups uncooked	6¾ cups cooked
2 slices bread	1 cup soft bread crumbs
4 slices bread, oven dried	1 cup dry bread crumbs

1 pound flour	4 cups
1 pound (2 cups) dried beans	6 cups cooked
10-ounce can condensed broth	2½ cups broth
3 cups cornflakes	1 cup crushed
1 cup uncooked couscous	2½–3 cups cooked
1 pound lasagna noodles	16–24 noodles
18 ounces peanut butter	2 cups
6 ounces pecan pieces	1½ cups
1 pound sugar	2 cups
1 pound brown sugar	2¼ cups packed
1 pound powdered sugar	3¾ cups
1 egg	¼ cup egg substitute
1 pound firm cheese (Cheddar)	4 cups shredded
1 pound hard cheese (Parmesan)	3 cups grated
4 whole large eggs	1 cup
7–8 egg whites	1 cup
1 pound frozen corn	1⅔ cups kernels
10 ounces frozen green peas	1½ cups
10 ounces frozen peppers and onions	2¼ cups
10-ounce package frozen vegetables	1½ cups
16 ounces frozen tortellini	3 cups cooked
1 pound frozen potato wedges	3 cups cooked
1 pound hash brown potatoes	2½ cups cooked

Food Doneness Chart

How can you tell when food is done? One way is to check the appearance: ground beef will have no trace of pink and fish will flake easily with a fork. However, the safest way to ensure that food is cooked all the way through is to test the internal temperature. Insert a meat thermometer into the thickest part of the meat, without touching any bone. Here are the internal doneness temperatures for various types of food:

Food	Temperature
Ground Beef	165°F
Whole Chicken	160°F
Chicken Thighs	160°F
Chicken Breasts	170°F
Pork	165°F
Steak, Medium Rare	145°F
Steak, Medium	160°F
Steak, Well Done	170°F

Pepper Identification Charts

▼ **CAPSICUM FRUTESCENS**

Name	Color	Heat Level (Scoville Heat Units)	Average Size
Tabasco	light yellow, ripens red	30,000–50,000 SHU	1–1.5" long, 1 cm wide
Thai Bird's Eye	green, ripens to red	50,000–100,000 SHU,	1" long, .5 cm wide
Piri Piri	green, ripens to purple or red	50,000–175,000 SHU	4" long, 1" wide
Malagueta	green, ripens to red	60,00–100,000 SHU	2" long, .5" wide
Japone	red	20,000–25,000 SHU	1–3.5" long, .5" wide
Bangalore Torpedo	lime green, ripens to red	16,000–50,000 SHU	5" long, .5" wide
Dagger Pod	green, ripens through orange to red	30,000–50,000 SHU	4" long, .5" wide
Kambuzi/Malawian	yellow, orange, red	50,000–175,000 SHU	1–1.5" long, 1.5" wide

▼ **CAPSICUM CHINENSE**

Name	Color	Heat Level (Scoville Heat Units)	Average Size
Habanero	green, ripens to orange or red	200,000–300,000 SHU	1–1.5" long, 1–1.5" wide
Scotch bonnet	green, ripens to bright orange and red	100,000–350,000 SHU	1–1.5" long, 1–1.5" wide
Naga Jolokia (Ghost Pepper)	green, ripens to deep red	800,000–1,000,000 SHU	2.5–3" long, 1–1.5" wide
Madame Jeanette	yellow, bright red	175,000–225,000 SHU	2.5" long, 1–1.5" wide
Hainan Yellow Lantern	yellow	175,000–350,000 SHU	2" long, 1" wide
Aji Dulce	green, ripens to red	200,000–350,000 SHU	1" long, 2" wide
Facing Heaven	bright red	200,000–500,000 SHU	2.5" long, 1.5" wide
Datil	dark yellow and orange	200,000–300,000 SHU	3" long, .5" wide
Habanero Red Savina	red	350,000–575,000 SHU	2" long, 1.5" wide
Jamaican Hot Chocolate	chocolate brown when ripe	100,000–200,000 SHU	2.5" long, 1.5" wide
Paper Lantern Habanero	lime green, orange, bright red	300,000–500,000 SHU	2" long, .5–1" wide
Aji Limo	yellow, ripens through purple and orange to red	50,000–60,000 SHU	2" long, 1.5" wide

▼ **CAPSICUM ANNUUM**

Name	Color	Heat Level (Scoville Heat Units)	Average Size
Jalapeño	green, ripens to red	2,000–5,000 SHU	2.5–3" long, 1–1.5" wide
Poblano	dark, deep green	1,000–2,000 SHU	4.5" long, 1.5–2" wide
Anaheim	light green	500–2,500 SHU	6–7" long, 1.5–2" wide
New Mexico	dark green, ripens to bright red	1,000–1,500 SHU	4–6" long, 1–1.5" wide
Serrano	green, ripens to red	8,000–22,000 SHU	3" long, .5" wide
New Mexico Big Jim	green, ripens to red	500–1,000 SHU	8–10" long, 2.5–3" wide
Casabella	yellow, red	1,500–4,000 SHU	1.5" long, .5" wide
Bola	red	1,000–2,500 SHU	1.5" long, 1.5" wide
Cayenne	red	30,000–50,000 SHU	4" long, .5-1" wide
Charleston Hot	green, ripens to bright orange	80,000–100,000 SHU	3" long, .5" wide
Cherry Bomb	green, ripens to bright red	2,500–5,000	2" long, 3" wide
De Arbol	red	15,000–30,000 SHU	3" long, .5" wide
Fresno	green, ripens to bright red	3,000–8,000 SHU	3" long, 1" wide
Goat Horn	green, ripens to bright red	5,000–8,000 SHU	5–6" long, 1" wide
Hungarian Yellow Wax	yellow, ripens to orange-red	2,000–4,000 SHU	5" long, 1" wide
Pepperoncini	green, ripens to red	100–500 SHU	3.5" long, 1" wide
Piquin	red	30,000–40,000 SHU	1" long, .5" wide
Padron	green	1000–1,500 SHU	4" long, 1–1.5" wide
Shishito	green, ripens to red	1,000–2,000 SHU	3.5" long, .5–1" wide
Thai Dragon	green, ripens to red	75,000–100,000	2–3" long, .5" wide

▼ CAPSICUM PUBESCENS

Name	Color	Heat Level (Scoville Heat Units)	Average Size
Rocoto	green, ripens to red	225,000–350,000 SHU	2–3" long, 1" wide
Manzano	green, ripening to yellow, orange, and red	12,000–30,000 SHU	1.5–2" long, .5–1" wide

▼ CAPSICUM BACCATUM

Name	Color	Heat Level (Scoville Heat Units)	Average Size
Aji	yellow, ripens to orange	40,000–50,000 SHU	4" long, 1" wide
Aji Cereza	bright red	70,000–80,000 SHU	1" long, 1" wide
Peppadew	green, ripens to bright red	1,000–5,000 SHU	1" long, 1" wide
Brazilian Starfish	red	5,000–20,000 SHU	1" long, 2" wide
Christmas Bell	red	100–500 SHU	2" long, 1.5" wide

Standard U.S./Metric Measurement Conversions

VOLUME CONVERSIONS

U.S. Volume Measure	Metric Equivalent
⅛ teaspoon	0.5 milliliters
¼ teaspoon	1 milliliters
½ teaspoon	2 milliliters
1 teaspoon	5 milliliters
½ tablespoon	7 milliliters
1 tablespoon (3 teaspoons)	15 milliliters
2 tablespoons (1 fluid ounce)	30 milliliters
¼ cup (4 tablespoons)	60 milliliters
⅓ cup	90 milliliters
½ cup (4 fluid ounces)	125 milliliters
⅔ cup	160 milliliters
¾ cup (6 fluid ounces)	180 milliliters
1 cup (16 tablespoons)	250 milliliters
1 pint (2 cups)	500 milliliters
1 quart (4 cups)	1 liter (about)

WEIGHT CONVERSIONS

U.S. Weight Measure	Metric Equivalent
½ ounce	15 grams
1 ounce	30 grams
2 ounces	60 grams
3 ounces	85 grams
¼ pound (4 ounces)	115 grams
½ pound (8 ounces)	225 grams
¾ pound (12 ounces)	340 grams
1 pound (16 ounces)	454 grams

OVEN TEMPERATURE CONVERSIONS

Degrees Fahrenheit	Degrees Celsius
200 degrees F	100 degrees C
250 degrees F	120 degrees C
275 degrees F	140 degrees C
300 degrees F	150 degrees C
325 degrees F	160 degrees C
350 degrees F	180 degrees C
375 degrees F	190 degrees C
400 degrees F	200 degrees C
425 degrees F	220 degrees C
450 degrees F	230 degrees C

BAKING PAN SIZES

American	Metric
8 × 1½ inch round baking pan	20 × 4 centimeter cake tin
9 × 1½ inch round baking pan	23 × 4 centimeter cake tin
1 × 7 × 1½ inch baking pan	28 × 18 × 4 centimeter baking tin
13 × 9 × 2 inch baking pan	30 × 20 × 5 centimeter baking tin
2 quart rectangular baking dish	30 × 20 × 3 centimeter baking tin
15 × 10 × 2 inch baking pan	30 × 25 × 2 centimeter baking tin (Swiss roll tin)
9 inch pie plate	22 × 4 or 23 × 4 centimeter pie plate
7 or 8 inch springform pan	18 or 20 centimeter springform or loose bottom cake tin
9 × 5 × 3 inch loaf pan	23 × 13 × 7 centimeter or 2 lb narrow loaf or pate tin
1½ quart casserole	1.5 liter casserole
2 quart casserole	2 liter casserole

Recipe Index

Index

We Have
EVERYTHING®
on Anything!

The Everything® list spans a wide range of subjects, with more than 500 titles covering 25 different categories:

Business	History	Reference
Careers	Home Improvement	Religion
Children's Storybooks	Everything Kids	Self-Help
Computers	Languages	Sports & Fitness
Cooking	Music	Travel
Crafts and Hobbies	New Age	Wedding
Education/Schools	Parenting	Writing
Games and Puzzles	Personal Finance	
Health	Pets	